RULES, ROLES AND RELATIONS

RULES, ROLES AND RELATIONS

DOROTHY EMMET

SIR SAMUEL HALL PROFESSOR OF PHILOSOPHY IN THE UNIVERSITY
OF MANCHESTER AND HONORARY FELLOW OF
LADY MARGARET HALL, OXFORD

BEACON PRESS *BOSTON*

TO MY FRIENDS IN
COLUMBIA UNIVERSITY
NEW YORK CITY

© Dorothy Emmet 1966

First published as a Beacon Paperback in 1975
by arrangement with St Martin's Press

Beacon Press books are published under the auspices
of the Unitarian Universalist Association

Published simultaneously in Canada by Saunders of Toronto, Ltd.

Printed in the United States of America

9 8 7 6 5 4 3 2 1

Library of Congress Cataloging in Publication Data

Emmet, Dorothy Mary, 1904–
    Rules, roles and relations.
    Reprint of the ed. published by Macmillan, London,
and St Martin's Press, New York.
    Includes bibliographical references.
    1. Social ethics.   I. Title.
[HM216.E4   1975]   170'.202   74–26764
ISBN 0–8070–1525–3

CONTENTS

PREFACE

THIS book grew originally out of discussions with members of the Departments of Sociology, Government and Philosophy at Columbia University, New York, in December 1960 and March 1962. My chief debt is to Professor Robert K. Merton. Whether or not this has turned out to be the sort of book he said he hoped that I would write, I trust that at any rate its dedication will convey to him and my other friends at Columbia, including those at Barnard College, how grateful I am not only for these conversations, but for the good times I have spent among them. I have also discussed a number of points in various contexts with my colleagues and students in the University of Manchester, and with members of the Epiphany Philosophers' group. The last chapter owes much to conversations with Tom Burns of the Department of Sociology in Edinburgh. Finally, Robert Merton and Samuel Coleman (also of Columbia) have read and commented on the MS. (They are not, of course, committed to agreeing with it.) I am also grateful to David Holdcroft for suggestions made in proof-reading.

I have written because I believe that moral philosophers and sociologists can have things of mutual relevance to say to each other. Also I have an impression that, while many of our most pressing moral problems arise out of the fact that we have to live increasingly in big organizations, most moral philosophy is still written in a vein which assumes that morality is a matter of face-to-face personal relations. I will yield to no one in believing that in the end this is what it is mainly about; but I also believe that the tensions and constrictions, as well as the opportunities, produced by our having to act in and through institutions cannot just be written about in these terms. If I had not seen a prior claim for a dedication, I should have liked to dedicate this book to administrators whose hearts are with the anarchists, and anarchists who can have a heart for the administrators.

DOROTHY EMMET

THE UNIVERSITY
MANCHESTER
April 1965

CHAPTER ONE

INTRODUCTION

To most of us, sooner or later, 'What ought I to do?' is seen to pose a problem. It may be a problem in a particular instance — where in this puzzling situation does my duty lie? Can I see any clear principle applying to it? Or, if more than one principle applies, which should have priority? These are problems for those who have firm moral principles. But there may be further problems behind these, which are not only difficulties in seeing how to apply what we think we already know about moral principles. Are our principles necessarily the right and only ones? We are aware that they are not shared by everyone in our own society, and certainly not by members of some other societies. Is there any satisfactory reason why they should be 'really right' even for us? And even if so, is there any justification for our trying to press them on other people, in moral criticism or moral advice? Further, a still more fundamental question: What is a moral principle, anyhow? What does it mean to say some rule is a *moral* principle? And what does it mean to be moral? Is it primarily a matter of principles at all, or is it not more likely to be a matter of feelings and attitudes, a kind of taste? And if so, is it the case that *de gustibus non disputandum*? Or is morality rather a prudential matter, a way of calculating what behaviour is most likely to conduce to favourable consequences to ourselves and others? And then, how do we decide what is 'favourable', and why bother about the others?

These, put crudely, are some of the questions which we ask when we come to feel that morality is problematic. And we may then wonder whether we can get any guidance on them from ways of studying ethics by philosophers, or from studies by sociologists of how people manage to live together.

People have been trying to find clues in the first of these for a very long time. The second, as a distinct and systematic study, is a comparative new-comer. It sounds a promising source, since, whatever else ethics may be about, it presumably has something to do with how people live together in societies. Yet when we look further into the work of sociologists, the next impression we get may be a frustrating one. It may show us morality as part of the way of life of a particular society without helping us to see what this 'relativism' means or implies for our own thinking about morals. Or it may suggest that if people have a particular position in a society of a particular kind, certain moral attitudes will result. And then what becomes of moral responsibility and moral choice?

We may also find what could be presented as a counter-attack on the part of philosophical moralists. The sociologists, it can be said, are simply describing the moral rules and attitudes people happen to have in a particular society and how they see these affected by the particular social relations in which they stand. This, however, is a description of what sociologists observe or infer to be the case, a matter of empirical fact. A person concerned with the question 'What ought I to do?' can find no answer in studying actual moral rules and behaviour, since no decision as to what *ought* to be done can be drawn logically from any statement about what in fact happens. It is a logically independent step, which must be taken in its own right. And if 'its own right' is defined by reference to rules or principles,[1] these must in turn be justified by a judgment

[1] For contexts in which it may be helpful to distinguish between 'moral rules' and 'moral principles' see below, p. 48 *n*. Generally the terms can be interchangeable.

that they *ought* to be followed. Indeed to say a principle *p* 'exists' in a given society will mean that people in that society think that they ought to follow *p*. The question still remains, 'Why ought they?' a question distinct from the mere fact that they do so or sometimes fail to do so.

This gulf between 'is' and 'ought', between questions of what is the case and judgments as to what ought to be done, puts a problem to which I shall be returning in later contexts. I only note here that whatever ought to be done ought to be done in a situation, and we like to think that any way of better understanding 'situations' and their facts should be of some help or relevance in making moral decisions.

This book is written from the conviction that it is justi-fiable to think this. We can accept the logical distinction between what is and what ought to be, and nevertheless think that reasons for moral decisions are partly at least factual reasons, so that empirical studies in sociology might help us in getting a better understanding of facts which can be taken into account in deciding what we ought to do. This may seem a fairly harmless thing to say, though it need not be trivial for all that. We can enlarge our vision of the factual situations in which we have to act, and in particular the networks of social relationships by which they are partly constituted. We can see further into the likely consequences of courses of action, and particularly be more alive to indirect and unintended consequences which may be the unwanted by-products of our intended acts. Sociolo-gists are particularly interested in tracing unintended con-sequences, since they train themselves to think not only in terms of unilinear strands of cause and effect, but in terms of reciprocal actions and reactions within multiple systems of relations. And if we can see more of the likely unintended, as well as the hoped-for and intended, conse-quences of an action we may be in a better position to decide whether we ought to do it.

Yet it may be said that however valuable this enlargement of our vision may be in the *applications* of ethics, in deciding how to act in actual situations, it would still leave the *theoretical* questions of ethics where they were. For instance, suppose one is a utilitarian, concerned to judge what is right or wrong by estimating the happiness which might be produced by different courses of action. Obviously it is useful as well as important to be able to see further into the probable unintended as well as the intended consequences of our acts, and if sociological enquiries give us the means of doing so, it is only prudent to avail ourselves of them. We might even say that we ought to do so (though a strict utilitarian might raise an eyebrow at the 'ought'). Yet however much this may enlarge our view of the reasonably foreseeable consequences of our actions, we still cannot see *all* the consequences, direct and indirect. And, more important still, this does nothing whatever to tell us whether or not we should be utilitarians at all; it only says that if, on whatever grounds one decides what ethical theory to adopt, we decide to be utilitarians, then some sociological knowledge can help us to be better utilitarians in practice.

So the question of whether a sociological interest can make any difference in principle to our theoretical understanding of ethics still remains. This is more controversial than the other consideration, important though that is in its own way, of whether it may help us in the practical applications of whatever ethical theories we happen to have.

I believe that a sociological interest can in fact affect our theory, though in an indirect way, and I shall be concerned with trying to show how this can be. It may not supply us with what could properly be called an ethical theory, but it may give us a 'general orientation' (the phrase is Professor Merton's, used in a different connection) in the light of which certain ways of looking at ethics become more plausible than others. Of course we have then to go further, and ask whether the 'general orientation' supplied by sociology is itself plausible. Similarly, I shall be arguing that there can be a reciprocal approach from the side of ethics. Do certain ways of looking at sociology become more, and some less, plausible in the light of what we think about ethics? In that case, similarly, the plausibility of what we think about ethics will need defending.

This suggests that there are considerations by which both sociology and ethics can be justified in their own right, and that each contains independent arguments for its theories. But it also suggests that they are not so completely independent and autonomous that what goes on in the one has no relevance to what goes on in the other. There may be some sociological questions which are also in part ethical questions and vice versa. The inference to be drawn, if I am right, is that a sociologist may be a better sociologist by being a reasonably sophisticated moralist, and a moralist may be a better moralist if he can enlarge his vision through a 'general orientation' gained from an interest in sociology. It may even be that the combination of the two interests may contribute something to understanding the situations in which we ask the painful substantive question 'What ought I to do?'

That there may be common ground to ethics and sociology might, we have said, be expected, since both have a common starting-point in the fact that people have to live with each other. (So in the beginning of our tradition Aristotle's *Politics* is not only a complement to his *Ethics*, but also a foundation book in sociology.) Yet they may be said to take off from this territory and survey it in different ways. Sociology, passing through a descriptive study of social action in human groups, looks for recurrent patterns in such actions, tries to see how far the ways people behave are explicable by their membership and position in social groups, and seeks for concepts in which this point of view can be organized and presented theoretically. Ethics passes from practical prescriptions about right and wrong to attempts at seeing whether anything can be said in general about what it means for actions to be right or wrong, and to considering relations between the concepts in which moral life can be discussed. The former could be a theoretical study based on descriptions of facts; the latter a theoretical study of what is implied by making prescriptions concerning what ought or ought not to be done.

Certainly there is this distinction: 'fact' and 'value', 'is' and 'ought' are not assimilable to each other. But neither do they inhabit different worlds: we are continually haunted by ways in which 'facts' are value laden, and are relevant to questions of what ought to be done. Sociologists are concerned with social situations, and these, we shall see, need more than reference to mere fact for their description. Moralists ask questions about what ought to be done, also in situations, where 'the facts of the situation' are relevant in some debatable way, and where what constitutes the 'situation' can be differently defined according to the range of human relationships taken into account. Again, the interest in each case may be different, but the common territory looks like not just a common point of departure, but a tangled undergrowth of facts and values through which both have to cut their way, and their paths may sometimes cross.

Sociologists get into the undergrowth because the social facts with which they are concerned are not just descriptions of physical actions, say, one man grasping another man's hand and then letting go, but of actions which indicate notions of what is proper as well as effective in their particular contexts; a handshake as a token of welcome, or reconciliation. Patterns of social action are not just regularities in how people are found to behave, but in how they are found to behave in part at least because of ideas they may have about what is useful, proper, the thing to do. These ideas, 'norms' in sociological terminology, may not always be regarded, but neither are they entirely disregarded. If they were, we might have an aggregate of individuals, but not a human society. This is both empirically so, and also can be taken as part of the definition of a society. A society is a more or less ordered way in which people live together, where the 'order' depends on their being able to entertain generally fulfilled expectations about how others should behave, so that they can co-operate or compete with some reasonable forecast of the sorts of things others are likely to do. Animals and insects, of course, may also follow cues as to each other's behaviour, but the cues are probably present stimuli in, e.g., sight or smell rather than 'expectations', and surely not expectations as to how others are likely to think it is *proper* to behave. Thus the order of a human society is not just a matter of spontaneous conformity or the automatisms of instinct, whatever that may be. Human social order involves rules and conventions, even if it is not just a put-up job. Human beings, we say, have minds and wills of their own; or if that sounds too question-begging, let us say that they are not born fully socialized, but have to be educated into a social way of life, and there are always liable to be occasions when they will put their own feelings and interests before what they have been taught. So a society will go on maintaining inducements to certain kinds of action and deterrents to others even after the period of formal training has been left behind. This is not only because a society is an ordered way in which people live together and do things together, and the order cannot just be left to look after itself. It is also because no individual member of the society could carry out his purposes unless he had some dependable knowledge of how other people were likely to act. This can be put by saying that social action depends on there being mutual reciprocal expectations as to how people are likely to act, and on these expectations not being too often disappointed. Hobbes saw this in his own way; how A will act towards B will depend partly at least on how he expects B to act

B

towards him. Here there are three broad possibilities: (1) the expectation of what we may call anarchic aggressiveness — Hobbes' *bellum omnium contra omnes* — in which A must always look on B as a potential enemy who may attack him. In such a state of anarchic aggressiveness there are no rules; or if there are, in the sense of Hobbes' Laws of Nature, they will be more honoured in the breach than the observance in the absence of any secure reciprocal expectations that they will be generally observed. So in this case, again to quote Hobbes, 'there is no place for industry; because the fruit thereof is uncertain: and consequently no culture of the earth; no navigation, nor use of commodities that may be imported by sea; no commodious building; no instruments of moving and removing such things as require much force; no knowledge of the face of the earth; no account of time; no Arts; no Letters; no Society; and which is worst of all, continual fear, and danger of violent death; and the life of man, solitary, poor, nasty, brutish and short'.[1] As Hobbes saw, the pure model of anarchic aggressiveness would not represent anything stable enough to be 'society' at all.

(2) Secondly, there could be what we may call structured aggressiveness, of which the model is a competitive two-person game of skill. Here A's acts will take account of how he expects B to act, on the assumption that each is trying to wrest advantages from the other *within the possibilities which are allowed by the rules of the game*. (The Theory of Games contains technical studies of how each side may work out strategies in relation to what the other side is likely to do.) The situation is deliberately structured by setting up rules which limit not what is physically possible, but what is permitted. Some limits are of course set by physical facts; no one can run chasing a ball down a field at 100 miles an hour — these are natural limits. Rules set artificial limits to what is allowed to be done.

---

[1] *Leviathan*, Chapter XIII.

Hobbes' view of the Social Contract suggests the transition from a model of a society in terms of anarchic aggressiveness to one of structured aggressiveness bounded by rules, with a Sovereign as umpire to see they are kept. The analogy is not of course complete; the point of the rules in a Hobbesian commonwealth is to prevent others from frustrating one's desire to live peaceably, rather than to set up a structure within which each party can try to beat the other. They are thus rules for the possibility of peaceful living and not rules for war; or in so far as there may be 'rules of war', such as Hobbes' fifteenth Law of Nature concerning the safe conduct of mediators, or Geneva conventions concerning treatment of prisoners, they are rules which presuppose that war is not the total or permanent condition of society. If there were to be literally and completely 'total war' everywhere at once, it would surely spell the end of human society. (Who, for instance, would look after the children?) Also perfect competition in a free market is an artificial model abstracted from a social background in which there are some non-competitive understandings — for instance, that contracts should be kept and are enforceable at law. And if Durkheim is right in *The Division of Labour*, even they would not be enforceable apart from some generally shared social feelings about honest dealing. Structural aggressiveness is thus not plausible as a total model of human society, though it can be the model of a game, or war, in so far as the nearest analogy to war (as Lord Wavell once remarked in a lecture on 'Generals and Generalship') is that of a very rough and dirty game. It represents certain patterns of human activities which presuppose a wider background, less aggressive than war or the mock aggressiveness of a game structured by rules.

Wittgenstein has indeed called attention to the great variety of what may be called games, and so in what may be meant by following the rules of a game.[1] Nevertheless,

[1] *Philosophical Investigations*, § 66.

among the 'family resemblances' in activities called games, must we not say that a game is something *bounded* from a wider context, so that some actions are and some are not part of the game, and in which the rules indicate these bounds? Even if, as Wittgenstein says, there may be games in which you may make up the rules as you go along, yet at each stage the rules will show that some things are in and some are out. And, as Wittgenstein also says, 'It is not possible that there should have been only one occasion on which someone obeyed a rule', so that even if, as he says, there may be games in which we *alter* the rules as we go along, the altering cannot be quite arbitrary and idiosyncratic to each player, or made at every move. The croquet in *Alice in Wonderland*, where the players all played at once without waiting for turns, and where the hoops were always getting up and walking to other parts of the ground, does not seem to have been an occasion on which Wittgenstein's test for the existence of a rule ('Now I can go on') would have meant very much; indeed, as Alice observed, you never knew if it was your turn or not.

Social life may not be as chaotic as croquet in Wonderland, but nor may it be as circumscribed as a game with rules. Even if we allow Wittgenstein's highly liberal interpretation of what may constitute a game, in the case of social life the boundaries defining what is and what is not part of the game may be much more difficult to draw. So also may be the description of what constitutes winning or losing. Nor are the situations in which the rules apply as systematically defined as are those of a game. (This is not to say that societies or social situations are not bounded, but they are bounded in different ways.) In spite of myths of social contracts and primitive lawgivers, whether human or superhuman, it is very unlikely that all the rules of a human society will be matters of deliberate contrivance. So models of structured aggression are only of limited application.

(3) We come, then, to the mixture of competitiveness and co-operation, of custom and contrivance, of planned policies and blind happenings which go to make up social life as we know it. It is not necessary, here at any rate, to express any view on whether human action is always self-centred or sometimes altruistic. Arguments about this may be not very profitable speculations about springs of action, or may turn, as Bishop Butler pointed out, on ambiguities in the notion of an action as done from an interest. We need only remark that in social life people sometimes compete and sometimes, for whatever reason, co-operate, and that they could do neither effectively unless they could count up to a point on what others would do. These fairly stable mutual expectations, which are the conditions of purposive action in any society, are only fulfilled where there are some generally accepted ways of behaving. Some of these indeed may be known to have been enacted officially as laws; others are likely to be customs and prescriptions for conduct which may never have been systematized, and of which the origin is obscure. In any case, sociologists are unlikely nowadays to concern themselves with the question of origins;[1] they will be content to observe how any society as a going concern contains various kinds of rules as to what is considered proper and improper behaviour. A society of spontaneous co-operators might exist without rules: are there rules in Heaven, or for that matter in a beehive? In other words, a spontaneously harmonious society might, as Aristotle would say, be one either of gods or beasts. It would not be human society as we know it.

To study human society is, then, to take account of conduct which is partly at least rule directed. It is to observe not just regularities in conduct, but *regulated* conduct.

[1] Their German forebears in the last century had no such inhibitions; they sought the origin of at any rate art and religion in *Urdummheit* (primaeval stupidity).

A rule is a directive that acts of a certain kind should or should not be done on certain kinds of occasion by a person, a certain kind of person, or anyone. It is not a command, which is an injunction to a particular person or group on a particular occasion, though a person may make a rule for himself for certain kinds of occasion.[1] Rules may be officially promulgated in a legal system or set of regulations; these, however, work within the context of wider, less formulated practices and pressures, which also have their rules, though these may not always have been deliberately and systematically set up. From one point of view, seen as observed regularities of conforming behaviour, they can be called customs; from another, in so far as to go against custom is held to be not only exceptional but reprehensible, they can be seen as social rules: 'this is how people ought to behave on such and such occasions'. Of these rules, some may be matters of morals, others of manners; at this level no clear distinction need be drawn. We

[1] D. S. Shwayder's book *The Stratification of Behaviour* (London and New York, 1965) came into my hands at a late stage in completing my own. Shwayder has a full and valuable discussion of the notion of rules and their kinds (pp. 233–280), well documented from recent work in philosophy. He defines rules as figuring where proficient behaviour is also conformative behaviour (not just behaviour that happens to conform). A rule supplies a standard of correctness of the behaviour, and gives rise to warranted or legitimate expectations on the part of other people. I do not think that what I have said here and in other passages is substantially at variance with the points Shwayder makes about rules. His book may be consulted for a forcible and detailed treatment of the whole question. See also Max Black, 'Notes on the meaning of "Rule" ', *Theoria* (1958), pp. 107–126 and 139–161. Black distinguishes between regulations (which are rules laid down by proper authority for a special purpose, e.g. the conduct of an examination or the parking of cars) and instructions, precepts and principles. A similar set of distinctions is made by K. Baier, *The Moral Point of View*, Chapter V (Cornell, 1958); he adds *mores* as kinds of conduct held appropriate in a social group and supported by unformalized pressures.

shall, however, be concerned later with seeing what characteristics a rule of the *mores* will have if it is explicitly seen
as a *moral* rule.   At this stage, we can note that rules of the
mores may be a combination of manners and morals, are
likely sometimes to be ambiguous, sometimes inconsistent,
and it may be possible sometimes to break them without
an umpire calling one to order.   Nevertheless, they enable
an aggregate of people to live as a social group.

The kinds of practice and pressure which serve to
structure a society, so that it is possible for people to entertain more or less dependable expectations about each other's
behaviour, stem from the fact that people are not just unique
individuals confronting each other as unique individuals.
There may indeed be a profound sense in which they are
just this, but if it were the whole truth society would need
to be an anarchic Utopia.   Empirically this does not seem
to be viable, and there may also be good ethical reasons why
it would not even be desirable.   People in fact meet one
another in a host of social relations.   There are kinship
relations, such as husband and wife, parent and child;
professional and trading relations; relations between officials and members of the public, between teachers and
pupils, between host and guest, between friend and friend.
And so on, and so on.   Where relations are of a sufficiently
recognizable type to be called by common names, the
persons entering them can be referred to not only by their
proper names, but by their roles.   Whether every social
relation should be described as a role relation may be a
matter of logic, as defining how a term is being used,
though we shall see later that this may also be put as a
material question with ethical implications; but whether
or not role relationships are seen as omnipresent in social
life, at least they form its recognizable patterns.

A role is a capacity in which someone acts in relation
to others.   It is, of course, a metaphor from the theatre,
where a role is a part assumed by one actor in a play where

others assume other parts. It need not, however, connote 'play acting' (though we shall see later that this charge may be levelled against 'role behaviour' by its existentialist critics). It does, however, suggest a way of acting in a social situation which takes account of the specific character of the relation, and which is considered appropriate in a relation of that kind, either for functional reasons or from custom and tradition. A role relation is therefore more than a purely physical relation.[1] This is brought out classically by Hume's question about the difference between a parricide and a sapling which stifles a parent tree:[2] 'Let us choose any inanimate object, such as an oak or an elm; and let us suppose that, by the dropping of its seed, it produces a sapling below it, which springing up by degrees, at last overtops and destroys the parent tree: I ask, if in this instance there be wanting any relation, which is discoverable in parricide or ingratitude? Is not the one tree the cause of the other's existence; and the latter the cause of the destruction of the former, in the same manner as when a child murders his parent? 'Tis not sufficient to reply that a choice or will is wanting. For in the case of parricide a will does not give rise to any *different* relation, but is only the cause from which the action is deriv'd; and consequently produces the *same* relations that in the oak or elm arise from some other principles.' Hume says what is lacking in the one case and found in the other is a *sentiment*, as an emotion of disapproval 'in the breast' of the observer

---

[1] I tried to bring out how the notion of a role has built into it a conception of appropriate conduct in a social context in my lecture *Facts and Obligations* (Dr. Williams' Trust, 1958); and especially how the 'Natural Law' view of the value of the human being could be read as a way of extending the notion of role to that of a human role in a universal moral community. I find a similar point has been made more fully, and with a good deal more precision, by A. I. Melden, *Rights and Right Conduct* (Blackwell, Oxford, 1959).

[2] *Treatise on Human Nature*, Book III, part i, § 1.

of the parricide. The emotion of disapproval need not only arise in the breast of an observer. It would no doubt have been felt too by the parent as he fell murdered. Participants in such situations, no less than observers, feel approvals and disapprovals, because they see them as *social* relations, i.e. not constituted only by physical facts of efficient cause, which is the relation on which Hume concentrates, but by psychological facts of mutual expectation, trust, affection, or the equally psychological fact of withholding these. So a role relation in a social situation has some notion of conduct as appropriate or inappropriate built into its description, as Hume saw very well in his account of the dependence of human society on the artificial virtues.

The concept of role is thus one which enters into the sociologist's account of a social situation. It is needed in describing the repeatable patterns of social relations which are not mere physical facts, and which are structured partly by the rules of acceptable behaviour in the society in question. But the concept is also of interest for the moralist when thinking about questions of right and wrong. We shall indeed be asking whether it is not a notion more deeply embedded in actual moral questions than theoretical moral philosophers have always recognized. What people think they ought to do depends largely on how they see their roles, and (most importantly) the conflicts between their roles. It may be a bridge notion between myself as an individual, with my proper name and my personal responsibility, and 'my station and its duties' in the institutional world of the society in which I have to live.

Sociologists, then, as well as moral philosophers, will need to be concerned with the kinds of rules which moral rules may be; and they will be concerned with actions in social relationships in which people carry out various roles. The undergrowth of facts and values through which each party is trying to find its way is thick with rules, roles and relations. Can each nevertheless cut his way through them without needing to cross the other's path?

There is a case for each expedition being independent of the other, and this must be examined.

CHAPTER TWO

THE ALLEGED AUTONOMY
OF SOCIOLOGY

WE can start from the authority of Max Weber, one of the founding fathers of modern sociology. His testimony can be taken the more seriously because Weber himself was a man of strong moral convictions and impressive moral concern. He insisted that a sociologist must learn to distinguish logically between factual and value statements, and be clear which he is making.[1] He insisted, because on the one hand claims were being made that, e.g., economics could be an ethical science with empirical foundations; and on the other hand he saw 'professorial prophets' using their lectures to put forward their own political, religious and ethical views in the name of science. His point was that 'norms' could not be derived from empirical social science; this is not to say that value judgments do not have a place in social science. On the contrary, Weber was well aware that sociologists were not only continually being concerned with describing values, but were also using values to define their problems. This was because he saw cultural events as not just any kind of happening, but as defined through the interests and values that gave them significance (this, he said, was as true of prostitution as of religion). A sociologist may indeed be concerned

[1] See especially 'The Meaning of Ethical Neutrality' and 'Objectivity in Social Science' in *The Methodology of the Social Sciences* (translation by Edward A. Shils and Henry A. Finch. The latter paper, which was originally a policy statement, written in 1904, for the *Archiv für Sozialwissenschaften und Sozialpolitik*, is of particular interest for this whole question).

to study this significance through the evaluations made by various social groups, and a great deal of Weber's own work consisted just in this. He saw this as a concern to diagnose and describe; this was neither to pass moral judgment nor implicitly to accept the values described. 'Understanding all' does not mean 'pardoning all', as if understanding of another's viewpoint as such leads in principle to its approval. Rather, it may lead at least as easily to greater awareness of the issues and reasons which prevent ethical agreement. That is to say, Weber is insisting on the *ethical neutrality* of sociology as a descriptive study. A sociologist has indeed his own ethical values *qua* sociologist, the values of scientific integrity, the scrupulousness that allows him to be neutral in his work. His personal values may direct his attention to a problem; they should not affect his descriptive analysis of it.

A still simpler view is maintained by G. A. Lundberg.[1] A social scientist as such is concerned with facts and with the rules of scientific procedure. That is, he himself has an obligation to maintain these rules, and he himself as a human being will have his moral views. But as a sociologist he is concerned to talk about what is and not what ought to be. If he is called in as a consultant to advise, as a sociologist he is concerned only with showing the most efficient means to whatever end may be sought, or more succinctly in 'merely predicting that a certain manipulation of factors in "what is" will result in something different'. True, this is not as callous as it sounds, since Lundberg and others who take a similar view are equally emphatic that a sociologist outside his social science may have his own moral values in response to which he may decide to refuse to supply technical advice on means to some ends of which *qua* human being he disapproves. But he stands firmly by the ethical indifference of means, and on the sharp separation of fact

[1] G. A. Lundberg, *Social Research* (New York, 1948), pp. 53-54. See also his *Foundations of Sociology* (New York, 1939), pp. 29-31.

and value. I do not know what Lundberg's own episte-
mology of values may be.[1] To Weber, values are a matter
of 'faith', by which he presumably meant that they were
not matters of scientific knowledge. It may not be necessary to hold an 'emotive attitude' view of values in order to
maintain a distinction between fact and value or between
what is and what ought to be. It is only necessary to be
able to distinguish between factual description and approvals and to be able to show that the factual and valuational aspects in any statement can be distinguished. This
latter proviso is important for those who want to maintain
the ethical neutrality of sociology, since their studies abound
in terms such as 'normal', 'integration', 'equilibrium'
which are 'normatively ambiguous',[2] i.e. it is difficult
always to see whether they are being used in a purely
factual sense, and, if so, what this is, or whether they have
built into them some implicit assumption as to a desirable
state of affairs. But even if we grant that this distinction
can be made, and that it is possible to give a valuationally
aseptic meaning to notions such as 'normal' or 'integration'
or 'social harmony', and that many sociologists succeed
in doing so, there still remains the question of whether
it is possible always to make a clear distinction between
factual means (a technical question) and valuational ends
(a practical moral or policy question). One adopts or
advises on not only means to ends but courses of action,
and a course of action combines technical considerations
with considerations of what people ought to be asked or
induced to do. Moreover, a sociologist's values may
influence what he sees as a problem to investigate, and still

[1] But cf. *Social Research*, pp. 100–101, where values are connected
with sensory discriminations, like the 'secondary qualities', 'cooler',
'sweeter', etc.

[2] To borrow a term of H. D. Lasswell and A. Kaplan in another
context, writing about political science. (*Power and Society*, Yale
Law School Studies 2, 1950.)

more, what would constitute a 'solution' to it. Suppose an investigation were set up into the incidence of juvenile delinquency in a certain place and time, and suppose it were ascertained that part of the difficulty was that there were too many children, either for the teachers in school to discipline the large classes, or for the policemen on the beat to keep an eye on them. Supposing it did not seem feasible, given the proportionate number of the adult population, vastly to increase the number either of teachers or of policemen, then the sociologist might say that among the alternatives one effective thing to do would be to reduce the number of children by, e.g., strangling a certain proportion of them. Jonathan Swift said much the same in *A modest proposal for preventing the children of poor people from being a burthen to their parents or country and for making them beneficial to the public*: 'I have been assured by a very knowing American of my acquaintance in London, that a young healthy child well nursed is at a year old a most delicious, nourishing and wholesome food, whether stewed, roasted, baked or boiled, and I make no doubt that it will equally serve in a fricassee or a ragout'. Among the incidental advantages, this would lessen the number of Papists 'who are the principal breeders of the nation', besides helping the economy, and bringing direct profit to the parents who bred and sold children for this purpose. The persons who had invited advice from the sociologist would no doubt indignantly answer that this was 'no solution'. That is to say, what people are prepared to accept as a solution is not simply a question of technically efficient means to a desired end. In one sense, infanticide might be a very efficient solution to the problem (after all, Hitler spoke of the 'final solution' to the Jewish problem). That people would not be prepared to stomach it might be a fact for the sociologist to take into account in considering the efficiency of this as a solution. But apart from this, would he be prepared seriously to say this would be a solution? And if he did so, would he in fact be neutral, or would he be making a value judgment in being prepared to entertain the possibility of such a callous solution (note the value-laden word)? So moral and social values can affect what are allowed to count as *means* to a solution of a problem, as well as affecting what is seen as the end to be achieved.[1] The distinction of morally neutral means, as a technical matter, and of ends as a matter of value judgment or emotional preference, is thus too simple. This indicates also that the distinction of fact and value is not the same as the distinction of means and ends. Some means may be considered objectionable not because they lead to 'unsought ends', whatever that may mean,[2] but because they would be the kind of thing one is not prepared to do.

Of course the verdict of the hypothetical sociologist might be a more limited one. He might not go so far as to recommend any course of action as means to the end, but confine himself to a diagnosis of the problem, by saying that the high incidence of juvenile delinquency appeared to be due to the fact that there were more children than the existing persons in authority could control — and leave it to others to recommend what might be done about it. Even so, I think it can be said that the sociological interest is not just a technical interest in establishing the facts of a value-free problem. To begin with, that juvenile *delinquency* is seen as a *problem* is a problem about 'norms' in the society concerned. 'Problem' here generally means a question, calling for a practical solution, and not only establishing what is the case, which would be a 'problem'

---

[1] I am indebted here to recollections of a discussion with Professor J. A. Passmore. That Professor Passmore should hold this view is the more significant in that he is prepared to allow a considerable ethical neutrality to the social sciences.

[2] Cf. H. A. Simon, *Administrative Behaviour* (2nd edition, New York, 1959), p. 65, who tries to define the distinction like this, though he indicates he is not quite happy about it.

in the theoretical sense. The '*problem*' of juvenile delinquency is not just the *incidence* of juvenile delinquency.
This latter can of course be approached in a purely detached
way, with no assumption as to whether or not it is a good
thing that the norms should be kept or not. There may be
factual objectivity within the investigation of a situation
defined in value-laden terms. Nevertheless few sociologists
are likely to keep up a sustained interest in investigating the
incidence of juvenile delinquency, much less get grants for
it, unless they also believe there is a practical problem that,
if juvenile delinquency has increased and is increasing, it
ought to be diminished.

Thus a sociologist's value judgments as to what he thinks
in important ways desirable or undesirable can suggest
questions for him to investigate, sustain interest and also
define the area of a problem by suggesting the need to look
at incidental and indirect effects of policies which may
otherwise seem desirable as efficient means to some given
end. Professor R. K. Merton has illustrated how this
could be so in commenting on the results of an investigation carried out by sociologists who were asked to study
the effectiveness of propaganda designed to encourage
people to buy U.S. War Bonds in the Second World War.[1]
This showed that the techniques of the radio programmes
pushing the drive played on certain fears and sentiments
(this was well understood and calculated by the script
writers). It might then be said that a 'value-free' investigator of propaganda need only be concerned to show how
these worked, and whether or not the result was to encourage people to buy bonds. He could say 'If these techniques of persuasion are used, *then* there will be (with a
stated degree of probability) a given proportion of people
persuaded to take the desired action'. His findings could be
used by any interested group, and their values would not be

[1] R. K. Merton in 'Mass Persuasion: the Study of the Social
Psychology of a War Bond Drive' (New York, 1946).

his concern, at any rate *qua* sociologist. But even *qua* socio-logist, his values may affect whether he is likely to leave the question there, or whether he will look into other repercussions of the propaganda drive, and if so, which. If he was himself interested in values of human dignity, 'he would not only have asked which techniques of persuasion produce the *immediate result* of moving a given proportion of people to action, but also, what are the further, more remote, but not necessarily less significant, effects of these techniques upon the individual personality and the society. He would be, in short, sensitized to certain questions stemming from his democratic values which would otherwise be overlooked. For example, he would ask: Does the unelaborated appeal to sentiment (which displaces the information pertinent to assessing this sentiment) blunt the critical capacities of listeners?' [1] He would also be interested in looking at the longer term effects of the continued exploitation of mass anxieties.

There is, then, a strong case that sociologists will have to concern themselves with moral values. This is clearly so when the results of their work are drawn on in making recommendations about social policies of which they may or may not approve. Here we might say, nowadays at any rate, they are in no different position from, say, atomic scientists. But in the case of sociologists, this is also a persistent problem from the nature of their subject matter, and arises even when their interest is at its most theoretical, sustained by what looks like purely scientific curiosity. Their subject matter is social relationships, and the applications of their work may directly affect ways in which other people's lives are controlled. Moreover, the tests of their theories, if they are to be experimental, will necessitate getting people to behave in certain ways, and observing the results so there is also a problem in the strategy of the enquiry. You can push atoms about

[1] *Op. cit.* p. 188.

c

and be beastly to bacteria — can you equally 'manipulate' people? And even where the tests are not experimental, if the sociologist is simply concerned to observe and analyse how a community lives, he himself as an observer is not entirely detached from any moral obligations. The observer of a group or community has himself a role in which he is related to the people he is observing, and, like all roles, this carries its obligations. Or, rather, he has two roles, that of investigator and that of guest in the society. Anthropologists in particular, who must learn to live in a relation of mutual trust with communities whom many of them come to call 'their people', have to work out the obligations of this role. How far can they let themselves be involved in the moral conflicts of the community?[1] How far can they publish their findings, and yet respect confidences (for instance, about the ritual practices of a secret society)? Such questions go beyond the intellectual question of how an anthropologist can learn to think sympathetically in terms of the categories and assumptions of the people he is studying and yet at the same time be able to switch back to his own critical and scientific categories and assumptions. For they are moral questions about the obligations of an observer to the people he is observing. And this is a problem which the atomic scientist does not have over his atoms. That is to say, the relation of the sociologist to his subject matter is a *social* relation in a way in which that of the natural scientist is not.[2]

[1] Elenore Smith Bowen's *Return to Laughter* (London, 1954) is a novel giving a vivid description of the dilemma of an anthropologist who had insufficiently prepared herself on this point — but I suspect this lack of mental preparedness is rare.

[2] On this, cf. A. W. Gouldner, *Patterns of Industrial Democracy* (London, 1955), pp. 268–269; where he speaks of his team's uneasiness about 'bureaucratically prying' into the privacy of the workers' lives. 'This is a real question to which there is no flip answer. We all argued the problem at length: what right *did* we have to intrude ourselves into others' lives? We could only say,

There are, then, the moral problems of the role of an investigator in a study which is concerned with how other human beings live. This does not mean that an anthropologist or sociologist cannot try to give objective and detached descriptions of the values and moral systems of the people he is studying without having to pass judgment on them. Other people's *mores* can be the subject matter of objective study as much as other people's diseases. But it does mean that he has to remember that what is an object of study to him can be a matter of passionate and even sacred conviction to the people he is studying, so that he ought to treat it with the respect due to other people's convictions.[1] This, again, is not to say that *tout comprendre c'est tout pardonner*. To understand a people's *mores* is to understand them, and to try to present them sympathetically in terms of their own interests and ideals; this is not the same as to approve of them, but it is to respect them. There is a switch of attitude involved here, but it is one which is surely perfectly feasible, through cultivating imaginative understanding of values other than one's own.

This is, however, an attitude which some critics of contemporary anthropology and sociology fail to understand,

finally, that we believed in our work and that we intended and hoped it would help people; or, more properly, that it would provide them with knowledge so that they could help themselves in their human predicaments. We do not doubt for a moment that this concern for individuals and their welfare, a sensitivity that no formal education in research could ever hope to instill, struck a spark and helped us to gain acceptance from the workers.' (This is an admirably candid acknowledgment that a concern to help people is not only something a sociologist need not be ashamed of, but that it can also be of positive value in his field work.)

[1] That one ought to respect other people's convictions is of course itself to make a moral judgment, and so would it be to claim that one need not respect them. (One may add, however, that besides the moral point, a sociologist who does not respect people's convictions is unlikely to get their co-operation.)

and this can be illustrated by the confusions which have beset the use of the notion of 'function'. It is sometimes assumed that to try to understand a system of *mores* in terms of its 'function' within a given society is to adopt a conservative attitude in which the given practices (witchcraft, for instance) are approved because they help the society to continue as a going concern, i.e. 'function' may be uncritically taken as value laden.[1] This need not be so at all. To say that a certain practice has a certain 'function' is incomplete. It can have a function only in relation to the context, of some purpose, system or interest to which it can be shown to contribute. Granted the existence of one of these, the item can then be said to have a function in contributing to its maintenance. So a practice may be 'functional' from the point of view of some interests in a society, and 'disfunctional' from the point of view of others.[2] It is, however, fair to say that when no purpose or interest to which the practice may contribute is stated, and when the expression 'the function of . . .' is used *tout court*, the assumption can generally be made that the context is the maintenance of the total complex.[3] So 'functional' ways

[1] See, e.g., G. Myrdal, *The American Dilemma*, vol. ii (New York, 1944), pp. 1015 *sq.* Also M. Polanyi, 'On the Introduction of Science into Moral Subjects', *Cambridge Journal*, vol. vii, no. 4.

[2] For a further discussion of the questions involved, see my *Function, Purpose and Powers*, esp. Chapters III and IV (London, 1958). Also R. K. Merton, *Social Theory and Social Structure*, 2nd edition, Chapter I (Free Press, Glencoe, Ill., 1957).

[3] Sometimes the complex may be a symbiosis which has established itself. *The New Yorker* quotes from a journal *Behaviour*. 'Domestic cats reared without access to the street develop a pathological timidity, attributable to the escape drive being released by stimuli which would otherwise be subliminal. I suggest that in European and American cities dogs and cats form a commensality in which the cats provide the stimuli releasing the chasing instinct of dogs, and dogs the stimuli releasing the flight instinct of cats, thus mutually satisfying otherwise starved drives.' On which *The New Yorker* comments 'You have to justify cities *somehow*'.

of thinking get the reputation of being conservative. But here, too, we must distinguish between the statement that 'x has a function in context C', as simply meaning 'x has such and such consequences in a given systematic context C' (the reference to a systematic context distinguishing such statements from mere statements of cause and consequences),[1] and the approval of the whole complex of activities. Nor need there be assumed implications that there could be no substitute for x, or that C would collapse if x was changed.

Nevertheless, most people want their societies to continue, however much they may want them changed in some respects. In fact this is an assumption so taken for granted that we are probably hardly aware when we make it. A sociologist is, however, interested in this as an explicit problem: how does a society manage to continue with some sort of stability, and adjust itself to changes? After all, the members of the society are individuals with minds and wills of their own, who can be recalcitrant, so that we cannot just assume natural harmonies as taking care of social stability. So he tends to take for granted that the stability and survival of the society is desirable — surely a very natural assumption, and if it be called a 'conservative' point of view, it is 'conservative' in the literal, etymological sense, and not in any party political sense. The late S. F. Nadel went so far as to say that an interest in these values was 'grounded' in the approach itself. 'Integration, regularity, stability, permanence, are all requirements of society as we conceive it; their disappearance means the dissolution of that very entity, society, and their strength or weakness, a measure of social existence. Thus in analysing any society we cannot but assess its capacity to achieve stability and continuity, to function smoothly and in an integrated

---

[1] 'Functions' in this sense can be causative when consequences reinforce motives to continue an activity. See below, p. 129, for a discussion of this.

fashion, and on this basis evaluate its adequacy.'[1]   He goes
on to say that this need not mean that we assume that
whatever is is right; in fact anthropologists will 'speak of
goals achieved at the cost of others, and of the price societies
pay for the aims they set themselves.   But here we can
no longer rely upon "grounded" value judgments: whether
social stability and national glory achieved at the cost of
human suffering are worth the price, whether relief from
tension through hunting down scapegoats represents a
"good" adjustment to existing conditions, these and similar
questions are answerable apparently only in terms of private
convictions — about war and peace, individual dignity, or
human happiness.'

The conclusion can be drawn that, while terms like
'stability', 'harmony', 'integration', even 'social health'
may sometimes be being used descriptively to denote a
state of society in which there is absence of conflicts, or
successful resolution of conflicts, they may also sometimes
be 'value laden', as implying that such a state is desirable.
But is it always desirable?   Should we approve of 'integration' in a Nazi Germany, or stability in an *apartheid* South
Africa?   Those who accuse sociology and anthropology of
being inherently 'conservative' in moral and political outlook have failed to see that this distinction can perfectly
well be made if one is careful about it.[2]

Indeed, it is a good rule of method to avoid using active
verbs with abstract nouns.[3]   Sociology and anthropology

[1] *Anthropology and Modern Life*.   Inaugural lecture, Australian
National University (1953), p. 17.

[2] It is not only people writing about sociology who sometimes fail
to be careful, and who write as though the perpetuation of an institution was *ipso facto* desirable.   My colleague Mrs. Barbara Rodgers has
told me of the Report of a home for unmarried mothers which
remarked, 'How sad it will be if after all these years of devoted service
this home has to close for lack of girls needing help'.

[3] Prof. L. J. Russell drew my attention to this many years ago, and
I have never ceased to be grateful to him.

do not take up attitudes. They are taken up by sociologists and anthropologists, who may hold them consciously or implicitly, in a responsible or in a confused way. And if we consider sociologists and anthropologists whom we know, we find that their personal moral attitudes are more often likely to be liberal or even radical than they are likely to be conservative. The trouble may be not so much that they take a conservative moral attitude for granted as that they may assume that a liberal democratic outlook is itself part of science, and that therefore assertions made from this point of view are scientific and factual, and not 'value laden'.[1] There is good reason to believe that liberal values — truth, freedom of thought, critical approach to truth, tolerance and goodwill to others — are germane to the ethical obligations of the role of being a scientist. But this is not the same as to say that they themselves are 'scientific', if this means they are not values calling for convictions and decisions. The influence of John Dewey in America in particular has encouraged people to assume that critical scientific intelligence and liberal values and goodwill go together. The great figure of Pareto — an intellectual authority for Fascists and thinkers on the extreme right — should have taught them better. The most that can be said (and it is a great deal) is that a case can be made for saying that the liberal values are 'grounded' in the actual pursuit of science, in a way analogous to that in which Nadel said that a *prima facie* approval of stability is 'grounded' in the pursuit of functional methods in sociology. There can be a slide from seeing that these are values which enter into the role of being a scientist to thinking that they are 'scientific' values, and then to talking as though they were objective facts and not values at all, in the sense in which other people's moral commitments are values. But

[1] See, for instance, I. C. Jarvie, *The Revolution in Anthropology* (London, 1965), Chapter I, who makes this charge.

they still remain commitments, and a sociologist may de-cline to make them.[1]

All this indicates that those working in the social sciences need to have thought about what they understand by a moral judgment and a moral commitment, if only in order to see more clearly where these can be avoided and where they cannot, and to be able to recognize them when they meet them. Where they cannot be avoided, social scientists will need to have some views on how they would set about justifying them. We are getting near to saying that they will need to take note of moral philosophy. How far the moral philosophers will help them is another story — the proof of the pudding must be in the eating.

There are, then, ways in which sociologists will be need-ing to make moral judgments, and in which they may be the better for a sophisticated awareness of what they are doing. They cannot avoid moral judgments since both their subject matter and their methods of enquiry involve human relations. Beyond this, they will also, especially if they are social anthropologists,[2] need to have thought enough about the characteristics of moral judgments to be able to recognize them in the societies they are studying. It might be thought that this is too obvious to be worth saying, or, again, that moral judgments are too obvious for it to be necessary to pay any special attention to their characteristics. Perhaps recent anthropologists in parti-

[1] Professor Michael Polanyi has a great deal to say in his *Personal Knowledge* (London, 1958) about how the commitments of scientists may enter into their heuristic processes of discovery. Does he suffi-ciently distinguish between how they enter here, and how they may enter into the checking of results, which is a more interpersonal matter, and where the struggle to get objective techniques is at its strongest?

[2] I am taking social anthropology to be, broadly speaking, the sociology of 'primitive' societies (i.e. non-literate societies without advanced technology). Increasingly, sociology and social anthropology are branches of the same subject, using the same concepts, and the discussions in this book apply to both.

cular have assumed just this.   I was lately asked to contribute an article on 'the relation between Ethical Systems
and Social Structure' to the forthcoming new edition of the
Encyclopedia of the Social Sciences.   I have to admit that it
came as something of a surprise to me to find that there was
practically nothing about ethical systems as such in the
recent sociological and anthropological literature I consulted, compared with the literature of the nineteenth and
early twentieth centuries where the ethical aspects of the
mores were a matter of passionate interest.   In contemporary work, plenty of attention is given to ritual and
religious systems, to political and legal systems, to kinship
and economic relations, but ethical systems *per se* are hardly
noticed.   No doubt this is because ethics, under the general
notion of the *mores*, is seen as permeating all these other
sides of life.   But if the distinctively ethical aspects of the
mores, as distinct from the aspects of etiquette, religion or
law, are not considered as such, we cannot see how these
distinctions are drawn, if they should be drawn at all, and
whether they are drawn in the same way in different cultures.   This lacuna in recent anthropology has been forcibly
pointed out in a paper by Abraham Edel, and he shows
detailed evidence for it.[1]   That what is to be diagnosed in
tracing out an ethical system is not an uncontroversial
matter can be seen by looking at books by three other
philosophers who have interested themselves in anthropology: John Ladd, in *The Structure of a Moral Code*,[2]
Richard Brandt in *Hopi Ethics*,[3] and Alexander Macbeath
in *Experiments in Living*,[4] as well as in another work by
Edel, *Anthropology and Ethics*.[5]   Each of these has a particular view of what constitutes an ethical system, and

---

[1] 'Anthropology and Ethics in Common Focus', *Journal of the
Royal Anthropological Society* (1962), vol. 92, pt. I, pp. 55–72.
[2] Harvard University Press, 1957.
[3] Chicago University Press, 1954.   [4] London, 1952.
[5] New York, 1959 (in collaboration with May Edel).

illustrates it by seeing how it measures up to the moral judgments of people of alien cultures. There is a distinction here; philosophers may start from a logical view of what constitutes an ethical proposition, and then only allow as ethical by definition those propositions that conform to this. In that case, the guidance they would give to an anthropologist would be a recommendation as to what he should be looking for in looking for an ethical system. On the whole this is the approach of Ladd and Brandt. (An anthropologist could challenge the recommendation by entering into the logical argument about what constitutes an ethical proposition — or of course he could choose to ignore it.) Or philosophers may start from a general view of the function of morality, a function which they think must be fulfilled in some way in any society (this is an empirical 'must', concerning the viability of a society), and try to specify further the characteristics of ethical systems by seeing how these functions are fulfilled in various societies. This is broadly the approach of Macbeath and Edel.

Since there is no ethical theory,[1] or even ethical terminology, which is agreed and non-controversial, both of these approaches can be defended. The conclusion for a sociologist or anthropologist is that he needs to be aware that what makes particular notions ethical notions is not self-evident. He therefore needs to do some thinking about how ethical notions are best described and distinguished. Moral philosophers may be able to help him; here again, the proof of the pudding is in the eating. Whether he in turn can help the moral philosopher is a question we can ask when we have considered the alleged 'autonomy of ethics'.

[1] Ethical *theory*, on a general level; the diversity of substantive morals is of course also a problem, but a different one.

CHAPTER THREE

THE ALLEGED AUTONOMY
OF ETHICS

WE have noted a common starting-point for both sociology and ethics in the fact that people need to live in social relationships with each other, not only for survival but if they are to carry out any of the characteristically human enterprises. We have also noted that a description of social relationships is not merely a description of physical facts, but involves reference to mutually and commonly held expectations as to how people should behave and of the social significance of their actions. 'Should' and not only 'will'; that is to say, forecasts of their behaviour are based on expectations of what they will think right or reasonable, and not only on inductive observations of actual behaviour; in sociological parlance, social behaviour will be interpreted partly with reference to 'norms'. That a norm is held in the society in question is a fact; that it is always observed is very unlikely to be a fact. A norm can be disregarded, especially when people think it would be in their immediate, if not long-term, interest to do so. Sociologists will therefore be interested in seeing how various kinds of sanctions, either formal or informal pressures, may be brought to bear to encourage wavering allegiance to the norms. In this context, ethical beliefs, their consequences and their means of reinforcement, will tend to be studied as elements in the processes of 'social control', where law, politics, religion are also seen as such elements. This may well be a reason why, as I have noted, sociologists give little independent attention to ethical beliefs and judgments *per se*, and may be an instance where a view is consequent on the interests of a method of approach. W. G. Sumner indeed, a pioneer of the sociology of the *mores* (a term which he was responsible for introducing into the literature), attacked the disastrous tendency of philosophers to treat morals as a separate category, alongside religion and politics; morals, he held, only makes sense with reference to 'something else', the 'something else' for Sumner being the need for social conformity for the sake of survival and welfare.[1]   *Mores* as Sumner used the term are not just customs; they are customs at one stage removed in reflection; 'popular usages and traditions when they include a judgment that they are conducive to societal welfare, and when they exert a coercion on the individual to conform to them, although they are not co-ordinated by any authority'.[2] *Mores* are thus here seen as capable of being internalized, i.e. a person may come to believe that he should observe them apart from external and overt pressures. Also they are broadly believed to make for 'societal welfare' (even if, as a matter of fact, they do not). By building this second requirement into his definition of *mores*, we can ask whether Sumner is in fact free of a 'second order' theory about the nature of morality. And if so, is this a step into moral philosophy?

It is indeed such a step, because by saying the *mores* are customs which serve or are thought to serve welfare, he has introduced a reason which might be adduced if people ask 'Why ought we to do these things?', and so which can lead into an argument about the function of morality. We start from the empirical fact that every known human society has some things which are enjoined or forbidden, approved or disapproved. These may be prescriptions based on immemorial customs, or taboos. We can imagine

[1] *Folkways*, § 42 (Boston, Mass., 1907). It may turn out to be true that ethics only makes sense with reference to 'something else', but not in Sumner's sense. See below, p. 53.

[2] *Ibid.*, Preface, p. iii.

the elders saying 'These are things that ought and ought not to be done'; but it is easy also to imagine someone asking 'Why?' Professor Radin has exploded the notion that no one in any primitive society asks questions about the *mores*.[1] And in any societies we know, especially societies undergoing change, it is all too obvious that people will want to ask why these things ought or ought not to be done, and will either want a reason, or a 'new morality'. So the 'Why?' opens up a demand for reasons: why ought we to do x and not y? Any society has its legitimatizing reasons. 'Because it has always been done' may get reinforced by 'and our ancestors were wiser than we are', or 'and God commanded it'.[2] The former *addendum* is a claim for which our imaginary proto-moral philosophy may ask evidence ('How do we know they were wiser?'). The latter one looks like a statement of fact for which evidence may also be asked: 'Why ought we to do what God commands?', which might elicit answers, either of the 'Because we had better — or else' type, or of the 'Because God is good, and knows what is good for us' type. In any case, a search for further legitimatizing reasons has got started.

The statement 'You ought to do x because it is socially beneficial' is another of these attempts at producing legitimatizing reasons. It is an attempt on lines which are likely to commend themselves to people in a liberal scientific culture such as ours; but this should not conceal the fact that it is not just an empirical descriptive account of morality, but an attempt to legitimatize certain customs by reference to a general view of their function. And as such

[1] *Primitive Man as Philosopher* (New York, 1927).

[2] Pareto discusses under the name 'Derivations' the kinds of reasons people will give for moral beliefs (cf. *The Mind and Society*, vol. III, New York, 1935). He sees human beings as impelled to look for reasons, but perhaps does insufficient justice to the ways in which (even outside logico-experimental science) some of these may be more rational than others.

it must take its place as an ethical theory of a utilitariant kind. In other words, we are into moral philosophy; for a utilitarian theory, however plausible, is neither self-evidently true, nor universally accepted, so its merits have to be argued and its difficulties met. It is of course a type of ethical theory which is likely to have a strong appeal to empiricists, since it looks as though it could produce good reasons why some things ought and others ought not to be done by referring to facts.

Moralists interested in the possibility of ethics as a 'special category' will, however, not let the utilitarian get away so easily with his factual reasons. They will maintain 'the autonomy of ethics' either on what we may call 'non-reducibility' grounds, or on what we may call 'non-deducibility' grounds. The former would be the contention that the *meaning* of ethical terms such as 'right' and 'good' cannot be exhaustively reduced to non-ethical terms. The latter would be the contention that no proposition containing an 'ought' or other ethical term can be deduced from purely factual propositions. According to the former, if we are told that 'right' means what God commands, this has to be supplemented by an ethical assumption that God is good and knows what is good for us, or else we have to make a decision to accept whatever God commands as *ipso facto* right, however it may violate our other ethical feelings, because we hold God has a *right* to command: this could be called the Abraham-sacrificing-Isaac complex. (The other line of thought — that we had better do what God commands, or else — is a prudential concern, not one about commands of God as *right* and we need not bring it in.) Similarly, if 'right' is defined as 'conducive to social welfare', questions can be asked about what constitutes social welfare, and if *moral* well-being is cited as part of it, the definition is thus far circular. If social welfare is described entirely in terms of non-moral facts such as health and prosperity, which it may be presumed we generally want, then why should I be told I ought to pursue them, and it is right to do so, on the occasions when I am not in fact interested in them, and why need I be interested in them for other people? The words 'right' and 'wrong' are normally used to persuade people not to go to hell in their own way even if they want to, and seem to be giving a reason for not doing so. To say that a reason embodying an ethical term can be exhaustively translated into one in non-ethical terms was called by G. E. Moore 'the naturalistic fallacy'. 'Fallacy' is a strong word; the claim that it is justified has been strengthened by the other approach to the notion of the autonomy of ethics which I have called the 'non-deducibility' view. This is the contention that it is not possible logically to derive a proposition containing an 'ought' from premises of a purely factual kind, which do not contain 'ought' or some other moral term.

A first reaction might be that this is no more than we should expect, since deductive logic is concerned with getting pints out of pint pots; in other words no more should appear in the conclusion than can be extracted from the premises taken in conjunction. This needs examining. In a good deal of moral argument and discussion we do in fact find what are ostensibly statements of fact cited as reasons, even apparently as sufficient reasons, why something ought to be done,[1] e.g. (a) 'You ought not to hit him because he is smaller than you.' (b) 'Since you want to pass your examination, you ought to do more work.' (c) 'You ought to help her because, after all, she is your mother.' Instances of the first type can fairly easily be shown to depend on a suppressed premise about what is fair or kind, and this is clearly a value judgment and not purely factual. By a 'value judgment' I understand an expression indicative

[1] On this, see especially Stuart Hampshire, 'Fallacies of Moral Philosophy', *Mind*, N.S. LVIII, 1949, and Paul Edwards, *The Logic of Moral Discourse* (Glencoe, Ill., 1955).

of approval or disapproval, which carries the implication that what is approved of should be done and what is disapproved of should not be done if the expression is used in circumstances where action is called for. I have entered the qualification 'where action is called for', for there may be purely contemplative or appreciative value judgments, e.g., in situations where there is nothing that need be done except admire or enjoy ('What a wonderful picture!'). But where action is called for, it would be irrational to say, for instance, 'I look on road collisions as bad things, so I ought not to try to avoid them'.[1]

The second assertion (*b*), 'Since you want to pass your examination, you ought to do more work', is an example where an obligation follows from the fact that someone has a certain purpose or desire. It is a 'hypothetical imperative', stating that if you have this purpose, these are the means you ought to take if you are to achieve it. The 'ought' here has the force of recommending the reasonable course of action. It cannot be eliminated by producing a hypothetical proposition in the form of a prediction, e.g. 'If you work harder, you will pass your examination', or 'If you do not work harder, you will not pass your examination', since some industrious candidates have bad luck and fail, or just have not got what it takes to pass, and some lazy hounds in fact have good luck and get through.[2] Kant put this point about hypothetical imperatives, when he wrote 'Who wills the end, wills also (so far as reason decides his

[1] Other things being equal; there may, of course, be contexts in which we think we are justified in doing an action of a kind of which, generally speaking, we disapprove. In a recent incident, a member of the public helped the police chasing a criminal by ramming the escaping criminal's car. The Insurance Company gave a new car as a reward for this collision.

[2] There could of course be a probabilistic prediction: 'If you work harder, you will be more likely to pass your examination' which would not be falsified by failure. But in this case, there is no 'ought'.

conduct) the means in his power which are indispensably necessary thereto'.[1] We may query whether the particular means are always in fact 'indispensably necessary'. There might be other ways of doing it, or we may just be lucky, by which I mean that conditions of success can come to us by external causal processes which we have done nothing either to promote or deserve. But the operative words in Kant's formulation are 'so far as reason decides his conduct'. This says that in adopting the said means, the person is also adopting a policy of acting reasonably; he is not banking on luck. It does not mean that if he adopts these means he will necessarily be successful. The *ought* is thus consequent on a commitment to act reasonably. Of course such 'means to ends' imperatives need not be *moral* imperatives; the prudential *ought* is a recommendation that certain means are likely to be the most effective way of securing the end whatever it may be, good, bad or indifferent. When the course of action is judged in moral terms, the means need not simply be regarded as raising technical questions of efficiency, moral questions only being raised by the nature of the end pursued. (We saw this in considering the question of policy recommendations made by sociologists.) Hence recurrent uneasiness at the saying 'The end justifies the means'. In one sense, we might say 'Of course it does: how else could they be justified?' If we have decided as a serious moral decision that some end should be pursued, for instance that we should try to win a war, then we must be prepared to take highly distasteful means to do it. But does it follow that *any* means judged technically efficient must be accepted? It is at least arguable that some means would be so horrible and corrupting that we ought to refuse to take them.

We return to the logical question of the possibility of deriving statements about what ought to be done from statements of fact. We noted a third type of statement in

[1] *Metaphysic of Morals*, § 42.

D

which it looked as if this was being done, in statements such as 'You ought to help her because, after all, she is your mother'. The obligation to help is said to follow from the fact of parenthood. But the fact is not a mere fact; it is a fact of social relationship.[1] And a fact of social relationship is one about people occupying roles *vis-à-vis* each other. The notion of a role has built into it a notion of some conduct as appropriate. It thus provides a bridge in instances of this kind between factual statements about social situations and conclusions that something ought to be done in them. What is thought appropriate conduct may of course vary from one society to another; there will be some ways in which parents will be expected to care for their children in some societies, and other ways in others. But there will always be *some* notion of appropriate conduct in the role relationship of parent to child, and vice versa of child to parent. Some of these will be so taken for granted that people can speak of 'filial' and 'unfilial' conduct, and even of 'natural' and 'unnatural' conduct, as though such conduct was fixed not by social custom, approval and disapproval, but by the order of nature.[2] But social behaviour is always artificial, in the sense that it is not just unlearned or impulsive. It is informed by expectations to which people have been taught to conform, as to how they should behave in certain relationships and situations; this may come to seem 'natural' where the expectations are so strongly grounded in custom and so widely accepted that they have come to seem self-evident. (This may lie behind the claim to 'self-evidence' of intuitionist views of moral principles.) The grounding in custom does not in the least mean that such ways of behaving are 'conventional' in the sense that they are arbitrary, and that there is no

---

[1] Cf. above, p. 14, where Hume's well-known passage about the sapling and the parricide was criticized on these grounds.

[2] For the ambiguities in the notion of Nature used in ways like this, see below, p. 178.

good reason for them.[1] But the word 'convention' takes care of the logical point: when an obligation is ostensibly being read from the facts of a social situation, this is because a social situation is being understood as a relationship in which certain conduct is expected as appropriate to the roles of the people involved. The notion of *role*, therefore, I suggest provides a link between factual descriptions of social situations and moral pronouncements about what ought to be done in them. It has, so to speak, a foot in both camps, that of fact and of value; it refers to a relationship with a factual basis, and it has a norm of behaviour built into it which is being explicitly or tacitly accepted if the role is cited as a reason.[2]

John R. Searle in the *Philosophical Review*, vol. LXXIII, January 1964, 'How to derive "ought" from "is"', has argued that this derivation can be made in instances of promising. From the descriptive premise, 'Jones uttered the words, "I hereby promise to pay you, Smith, five dollars"', and 'Jones promised to pay Smith five dollars', and 'Jones placed himself under an obligation to pay Smith five dollars', one can pass to 'Jones is under an obligation to pay Smith five dollars' and to the conclusion that 'Jones ought to pay Smith five dollars'. It is granted that the conditions under which Jones utters the words are ones in which he is participating in the socially recognized practice of promising; he is not saying them as, e.g., a line in a play, and Jones must not be under a conflicting and more stringent obligation (all this is entered as *ceteris paribus*). But to participate in a social practice or institution is to accept its normative as well as its descriptive character. If Jones in fact promises, he is making the

[1] Some of the early Greek discussions of whether morality was 'by nature' (φύσει) or 'by convention' (νόμῳ) were bedevilled by so seeing the alternatives.

[2] Cf. my *Facts and Obligations* (Dr. Williams' Trust, 1958) on this.

performatory utterance of committing himself to an obligation, and showing thereby that he understands and accepts
a norm of social morality.[1]   That Jones said 'I promise' as
a performatory utterance (not just a statement of fact) is
presupposed in the statements in the premises, even if the
first premise ('Jones uttered the words "I hereby promise"') can be taken as a factual statement reporting that
he did so.   The *ceteris paribus* means that the obligation
stands unless we have some reason for supposing that it is
not binding.   Since this question can be asked, to accept
the validity of the performatory utterance of promising is
more than to utter a tautology.[2]   This is perhaps concealed
by the fact that we most of us understand and accept the
institution of promising.   Suppose, however, one were to
eat fish with a woman and discover that according to the
rules of her tribe, this constituted an offer of marriage.
Would one then be under an obligation to marry her?   (I
owe this example to Professor N. Smart in discussion.)

My general conclusion is that where an ethical proposition appears to follow from statements of fact, there is some
value judgment, explicit or assumed, lurking in the background, or there is a tacit commitment to accepting the
norms of some role or institution which is being referred to.
This supports the 'non-reducibility' form of the thesis.
Allowing background assumptions, the precise claim of the
'non-deducibility' form of the thesis may, however, be too
strong.   It has been claimed that an ethical proposition can
only be deduced as the conclusion of a practical syllogism
in which the major premise is another ethical proposition
and the minor premise a statement of fact.[3]   Thus 'You

[1] I agree with the comments of Professor Antony Flew on this in
Analysis, vol. 25, no. 2.

[2] Cf. I. McClellan and B. P. Komisar also in *Analysis*, vol. 25,
no. 2.

[3] For this view, cf. R. M. Hare, *The Language of Morals* (Oxford,
1952). pp. 56 ff.

ought not to hit him because he is smaller than you' could be spelt out

> 'No one ought to hit people smaller than themselves
> Johnnie is smaller than you are
> ∴ You ought not to hit him.'

In so far as we reason syllogistically, either actually or by implication, this is no doubt logically correct. But there are other patterns of logical deduction of a non-syllogistic kind, using propositional calculus and quantification theory, where an ethical conclusion does appear to be strictly deduced from a non-ethical premise. Professor A. N. Prior has produced some of these in a paper on 'The Autonomy of Ethics'.[1] His first example is of the form 'P; therefore either P or Q': 'Tea drinking is common in England; therefore either tea drinking is common in England or all New Zealanders ought to be shot'. This example, however, is as he says, 'contingently vacuous', in that the expression E, here rendered by 'ought to' in 'all New Zealanders ought to be shot', could be replaced by any other expression of the same grammatical type, e.g. 'think they are going to', and the inference would remain valid. This form of deducing an ethical conclusion from a non-ethical premise is not therefore very impressive. One of Professor Prior's other examples might, however, be more impressive. He gives us the inference

> Undertakers are Church officers
> Therefore undertakers ought to do-whatever-all-
> Church-officers-ought to do.

This also would be contingently vacuous in the sense that both 'oughts' could be replaced at once by the same replacement and we could have a valid inference of a non-ethical proposition, e.g., 'Undertakers are Church officers,

[1] *The Australasian Journal of Philosophy* (Dec. 1960), vol. 38, no. 3.

therefore undertakers are over 21 years old if all Church officers are over 21 years old'. Or better, 'the minimum age of all undertakers is not less than the minimum age of all Church officers' (so as not in effect to be producing a syllogism). But what about the deduction of the ethical proposition? It could be expanded to say that if undertakers are Church officers and if there are things that all Church officers ought to do, then undertakers ought to do them. This is of course put out in syllogistic form, with a hypothetical factual major premise and a minor premise containing a hypothesis about obligations, and then there would be no problem about deducing the 'ought'. But the point of Prior's example is that with the help of propositional (or class) calculus and quantification, it need not be so put out or be hypothetical. We can pass straight from the statement that undertakers are Church officers to the conclusion that something that holds of all Church officers will hold of them. But the notion that one of the things that may hold of all Church officers is that they have obligations draws on an ethical conception in the background of the inference. This is the conception of Church officers as a class of people who may have obligations.[1] And, as Prior owns, in the statement that undertakers ought to do what all Church officers ought to do the notion of the possible duties of undertakers is parasitic on the notion of a wider class of duties, namely those of Church officers. We need therefore to be able to entertain the notion of a wider class of people having duties in order to be able to say something in the proposition about the duties of undertakers. So I think it is still fair to say that a conception involving

[1] The concept in this case is one of a role, but need not be a role or only dubiously a role, provided we can presuppose a class of actions appropriate to the kind of person named; e.g. 'John is wearing spats, so John ought to do whatever people wearing spats ought to do'. There is still an unreduced notion of what is appropriate which is being invoked.

ethical terms is being presupposed in order to make an inference containing ethical terms, although it is of course introduced into the deduction as a substitution instance for the variable 'whatever holds of Church Officers', just as the non-ethical concept of 'being of a minimum age' might be introduced as another substitution instance. So, formally and in abstraction, the conclusion containing ethical terms can be directly inferred from a non-ethical premise, but this does not tell us how we were able to get an ethical term to introduce as a substitution instance in the first place. This is why I claimed that in such deductions some notion of an ethical or at any rate value-laden kind, is lurking in the background. This is not of course part of the strict entailment, considered just as such. It is, however, part of the background of language which makes it possible to produce this particular substitution instance. Moreover, we need not only a language containing ethical terms to make this inference (which is indeed obvious); we also need the concept of Church officers as a class of people with duties (note that this may be built into 'Church officer' as a role concept).

This suggests that the 'non-reducibility' aspect of the 'is' and 'ought' distinction is more impressive than the 'non-deducibility' one, since if we choose to ignore what is being presupposed as background these entailments can be found.

So, we should be chary of elevating the non-deducibility of 'ought' propositions from 'is' propositions to the status of a 'law of logic' and still more, of baptizing it into this status as 'Hume's Law'. Hume said in a famous passage:[1]

'In every system of morality, which I have hitherto met with, I have always remark'd, that the author proceeds for some time in the ordinary way of reasoning and establishes the being of a God, or makes observations concerning human

[1] *Treatise on Human Nature*, Book III, part i, § 1.

affairs; when of a sudden I am surpriz'd to find, that instead of the usual copulations, *is*, and *is not*, I meet with no proposition that is not connected with an *ought*, or an *ought not*. This change is imperceptible; but is, however, of the last consequence. For as this *ought*, or *ought not*, expresses some new relation or affirmation, 'tis necessary that it shou'd be observ'd and explain'd; and at the same time that a reason should be given, for what seems altogether inconceivable, how this new relation can be a deduction from others, which are entirely different from it. But as authors do not commonly use this precaution, I shall presume to recommend it to the readers; and am persuaded that this small attention wou'd subvert all the vulgar systems of morality, and let us see, that the distinction of vice and virtue is not founded merely on the relations of objects, nor is perceiv'd by reason.'

The last phrase draws on Hume's own view of empirical 'relations of objects' and of the limited function of reason in perceiving necessary truths. Whether there is also a wider sense of 'rational' in which morality may be rational is another question; the point to note here is that Hume is claiming that it is 'not founded merely on the relations of objects', i.e. knowledge of physical fact, nor 'perceived by reason' in his sense of the term. But, as A. C. Macintyre has pointed out,[1] Hume himself does not make a complete dichotomy between morality and the facts of human nature as he sees them. He is objecting to people who pass from statements about what 'is' to statements about what 'ought to be done' without showing the bridges by which this is effected, and no doubt in particular, under the name 'vulgar systems of morality', he is having a tilt at the ordinarily accepted eighteenth-century theological morality. Hume's own bridge notions in arriving at the

---

[1] 'Hume on "Is" and "Ought"', *The Philosophical Review* (Oct. 1959), vol. LXVIII, no. 4.

view that, e.g., rules of justice ought to be obeyed are notions of human interests and passions; his view of the 'artificial virtues' is in effect a form of 'rule utilitarianism'.[1] Such bridge notions — Macintyre cites wanting, needing, desiring, pleasure, happiness, health, as instances — are capable of bridging what 'is' and what 'ought to be done' because they can be given a factual content (there are things we want, need, like, etc.), and at the same time, needs, interests, desires, etc., generally speaking, carry the implication that we approve of their being satisfied. They can of course appear as terms in statements that simply report. It is possible to report that someone has an interest, i.e. to make a descriptive statement; it is also possible to say he has an interest with the implication that it is a legitimate interest, i.e., to make an evaluative statement. Whether a statement is being made descriptively or evaluatively is more to the point than the distinction of sheer fact (which is hard to arrive at) and value. It is also always possible to raise the question 'Ought I to pursue this interest now?' (even where it is a legitimate interest) and this is the ethical question, bringing in a moral value 'on the back'[2] of these other values. We do not define the ethical 'ought' with reference to any other interest or purpose. But we should have no use for it apart from these other values, which we claim merit consideration, though they are never morally definitive.

Those who contend for the sheer 'autonomy of ethics' are driven to making these notions in the last resort ethically irrelevant; as Kant said, they may belong to 'anthropology', but not to ethics.[3] If we desire happiness, that we ought to

---

[1] See below, p. 84.

[2] For this phrase, cf. Nicolai Hartmann, *Ethics*, Part I, Chapter I. (English edition, London, 1932. Translation by Stanton Coit.)

[3] Cf. the Preface to *The Fundamental Principles of the Metaphysic of Morals*, 'A pure moral philosophy which is completely freed from everything which may be only empirical and thus belong to anthropology'. (Note, however, the word '*only*'.)

do what will promote it for ourselves or anyone else only follows if we can judge that happiness is good; and it might be said that from the ethical point of view (because of the 'naturalistic fallacy' and the non-reducibility argument) it is a contingent matter, irrelevant to ethics because empirical, that happiness rather than misery is desired, either for ourselves or other people, or health rather than disease.

Can we really believe this? Let us look at what a *purely* autonomous ethics not dependent in any way on questions of empirical fact would be like. It would presumably have to be an ethics of pure principles; [1] if we ask for reasons for one set of principles rather than another, what sort of reasons could they be?

1. Principles could be said to be a matter of pure personal decision. In this case there might be tests for the sincerity with which a person held his principles, for instance that he was prepared to apply them to himself as well as to others, but no *reasons* could be given. Some existentialists appear to be saying something like this.

2. Principles could be made purely authoritative, e.g., as divine commands. If no reason, such as that God is good and knows what is good for us, is given, this becomes arbitrariness at one remove.

3. The principles could be said to be seen to be rational *a priori* principles, either by a consistency test such as Kant tried to work, or by an appeal to self-evident intuition.

[1] A distinction can be drawn between moral rules and principles, as by M. G. Singer, in *Essays in Moral Philosophy*, pp. 160 ff., edited by A. I. Melden (University of Washington Press, 1958), and in *Generalization in Ethics* (London, 1963), taking 'rule' as a prescriptive statement to the effect that an action of a certain kind ought or ought not to be done, and 'principle' as a more fundamental statement justifying rules, or as definitive of the character of moral judgments. In the next chapter this distinction will be important. I shall draw it by distinguishing between 'regulative' and 'constitutive' principles, but otherwise I shall follow usage in sometimes speaking of specific moral rules as 'moral principles'.

An appeal to self-evident intuition is vulnerable to anyone who claims that these principles are not self-evident to
him. Kant's appeal to consistency was an attempt to show
that the contrary principles produce inconsistency. 'Inconsistency' here is not logical inconsistency, the simul-
taneous assertion of *p* and *not p*, but producing a maxim
for action which defeats its own purpose. The classical
example is lying; a lie is only likely to be successful where
there is a principle which encourages an expectation that
most people most of the time will tell the truth. Otherwise
the lie will not be believed. But, as Kant himself found,
there are not many principles in which this test of the inconsistency of their opposites can be found. And the
inconsistency is one not of logical contradiction but of a
frustrating state of affairs, one which Kant said one could
not rationally *will*.[1] This means that some cognizance
must be taken of facts, in the shape of consequences which
are thought not to be rationally acceptable.

Is it in fact possible for a morality of absolute principles
to sit so loose even as this to empirical questions of fact?
One must of course allow that we have to consider the
facts of a situation at least so far as to be able to see that
it is one of a kind in which a principle is applicable, for
instance, that this is a piece of property belonging to someone else in order to apply the principle of not stealing.
But sometimes we may find that the situation is one to
which more than one principle is applicable — for instance,
the time-honoured examples of situations in which there
is a conflict between the principle that one should try to
save life and the principle that one should tell the truth.
It will not do to say that in a 'consistent' set of principles
such conflicts would not arise. For this is one of the ways
in which moral principles differ from the rules of a game.
A game is deliberately set up so that there need be no two

[1] On this, rather than the consistency test, as being the main point
which Kant saw, see below, p. 70.

rules prescribing that a move should be made in different and conflicting ways at the same time — or if such a possibility is discovered, then it must be necessary and possible to amend the rules. One may, of course, be in doubt as to which is the best move to make out of a number of alternatives all permitted by the rules, but that is a different story since whatever move is made no rule is broken. But in real-life situations, it is perfectly possible for there to be situations to which several principles are applicable, and it is only possible to keep one at the cost of breaking another.[1] This is because principles do not form a single pattern in the way in which the rules of a game do, and because, in real life, situations are not artificially limited so that these conflicts do not arise. If they are to be solved in terms of a morality of pure principles, and not by considering, e.g., consequences, both proximate and remote, there would need to be a hierarchy of principles on a clearly indicated scale. I do not know that any morality of principles has been able to set this up so as to give guidance in all possible conflicts; at most some principles are held to be more stringent than others, and it is held that some ought not to be broken in any circumstances. Indeed a morality of principles, if it is to be applied realistically, must be supplemented by Casuistry. 'Casuistry' has had a bad press, largely, no doubt, thanks to Pascal's *Lettres Provinciales*; its popular meaning is dialectical skill in finding reasons for wriggling out of principles when they are in-

[1] This could of course be avoided if there were a morality which contained only one principle. But if the principle were a specific one, e.g. 'Thou shalt not kill', there are many areas of life on which it would give no guidance, so it would not be a viable morality, though a logically possible one. If the principle were a very general one, such as 'Thou shalt love thy neighbour as thyself', it might be generally applicable, but at the cost of giving very little specific guidance. So, again, a viable morality could hardly contain only this principle. (On the status of such principles, see below, pp. 84 and 200.)

convenient. It used to be treated with more respect; the original title of what is now the Knightbridge Professorship of Moral Philosophy in Cambridge was the Professorship of Casuistical Divinity. In fact, casuistry is a necessary exercise in trying to determine the limits of principles in regard to new and varied circumstances, and in trying to resolve conflicts of principles.[1] Thus it does take circumstances into account — the possibility of disastrous consequences, for instance — but it is not fair to call this 'setting expediency against principle'. It is rather an attempt to see how difficult cases may exemplify more than one principle; or whether an original principle can be interpreted less narrowly so as to resolve the problem or avoid disaster. Any legal system must use this method, and so too must any morality of principles including, so far as conflicts arise, the most fanatically rigorist. Casuistry does, however, normally assume a responsibility to try to avoid disastrous consequences. In political decisions, in the case of a minister of state, this responsibility for his country is indeed an obligation of his role as a minister; it is not just a matter of waiving principle for 'expediency'. The concern to avoid disaster does, of course, make a matter of empirical fact relevant to deciding what ought to be done. It does so by making it a matter of principle that disasters, especially those involving other people, ought to be avoided if possible. But it is *relevant*, not prescriptively decisive. One *might* still say *fiat iustitia ruat coelum*.[2] In the end the decision lies between the principle that one ought not to incur disaster for others and the principle, e.g., that one should tell the truth. Casuistry can go some

[1] The best discussion of Casuistry I know is in K. E. Kirk's *Conscience and its Problems* (London, 1927 : numerous editions).

[2] I am inclined to say that the only maxim which would be an immoral one for a politician *in any circumstances* is *après nous le déluge*, since to adopt this is to be irresponsible. And a deluge is just what might come if the heavens fell.

way in making explicit further refinements of principles. It would, however, be impossible to produce a complete set of principles which covered every possible case in full specificity, for if there were such, there might have to be as many principles as cases, and then the principles would be of no use in giving guidance from one case to another; they would only be a kind of double entry. So in the end an element of moral judgment not fully specified by principles is inevitable.

To say that to try to avoid disastrous consequences could be a principle may look like blurring the distinction between a morality of rules and a morality of ends. If, however, principles can be rationally discussed (i.e. they are not just self-authenticating or arbitrary), reasons for them can refer to some policy or way of life or form of human relationship judged to be good. A principle will be a general directive concerning acts of a particular kind which specify this way of life; e.g. telling the truth is a particular specification of a way of life characterized by mutual trust; it is also a means to securing this. Or a principle may be a general directive not to do things which will make the way of life impossible, e.g. to avoid acts which are likely to incur disaster for all concerned. The latter is a corollary of the more general principle that one ought to take responsibility for the foreseeable consequences of one's voluntary actions. This obviously involves taking account of matters of fact.

Thus it does not look as though moral principles with substantive content could be established without paying some attention to questions of empirical fact. The Kantian attempt to present a pure *a priori* morality did not succeed in showing that substantive principles could be derived from reason alone. If principles are not to be arbitrary, simply authoritative, or purely formal, their *content* must come through a context of notions such as commendable ways of life, good to be achieved and the feasibility of achieving it, the kinds of human relation of which we approve, the interests of others as well as ourselves. All such notions are 'value laden' in having a reference to human attitudes, needs and ideals; they also [1] have a descriptive factual content. Thus they can provide bridges in the morass of fact and values. Those who contend for the 'autonomy of ethics' are right on the 'non-reducibility' claim that the reasons supporting judgments of what is right and wrong cannot be *purely* matters of empirical fact, for they presuppose beliefs about what is desirable, approved, appropriate, and the reverse. On the other hand, if moral principles are not derivable from pure reason alone, then the empirical facts of a situation are not only relevant to a moral judgment in the sense of enabling us to see that it is one in which a rule should be applied (e.g. that the goods in the shop window belong to someone else, so that the rule that one ought not to steal is applicable). Facts can also be relevant because they are seen in relation to people's purposes, needs, interests, happiness, ideals. Ethics may find its place in this value-laden context of human interests and purposes, especially as these are pursued in social relationships with other people. It is notions of this sort which can provide the 'something else' in relation to which ethics makes sense.[2] A moral value is not something on its own in a vacuum. It is 'on the back of' these other values (to use Nicolai Hartmann's phrase), concerned with how

---

[1] 'Also', but not only. Mrs. P. Foot in 'Moral Arguments' (*Mind*, 1958, N.S. LXVII) gives 'rude' as an example of a term where the descriptive meaning is established, so that to say an action is 'rude' can be asserted on evidence that it gives offence. But when 'rude' is used pejoratively, the value judgment that lurks is that to give offence is generally wrong. Moreover, the descriptive meaning of 'rude' has not always been so settled. When the rude forefathers of the hamlet slept in Gray's churchyard, they were not giving offence, as they might have done if they had been snoring in the sermon.   [2] Cf. above, p. 34.

they should be pursued, and whether they should sometimes not be pursued, remembering always that their pursuit happens in a world of social relationships. It is not necessary to make one interest paramount, as on the whole is done by Utilitarians; indeed, which interest should be pursued and when can be a significant question, calling for a moral *judgment* in a particular situation, and the notion of 'right' can be (what Sumner objected to) a separate category, not reducible simply to, e.g., 'expedient'. We can go thus far with the non-naturalists. I therefore accept 'the autonomy of ethics' not as saying that there may not be calculi with rules by which 'ought' propositions can be deduced from 'is' propositions (the non-deducibility claim), but as saying that no 'ought' proposition can be defined in terms of facts alone (the non-reducibility claim). Some value will be being invoked or assumed, as one which the facts acquire in relation to human purposes, interests, needs, and there will always be the further question whether these ought to be pursued. Morality may thus call for distinct categories, but it does not exist in splendid isolation. A judgment as to what is right has to be made in a 'situation', and a situation is comprised of facts seen as bounded and related to human interests, problems, or attitudes (so situations are said to be embarrassing, encouraging, hopeless, hopeful). The moral judgment has to take account of the 'facts of the situation'. A purely autonomous ethics, not in any way beholden to empirical facts or to our interests in them, would be, as Kant saw, an ethics of *a priori* principles, which would have to be both self-authenticating and incapable of conflicting. I have questioned whether morality can be like this; what place it has nevertheless for rules and principles needs further definition. They may be important, but not sufficient, guides to moral judgment. Thus, just as the investigation of the alleged autonomy of sociology suggested that sociologists might do with help from moral philosophers in thinking about the character of moral judgments, so too the investigation of the alleged autonomy of ethics suggests that moralists might do with help from sociologists in enlarging their understanding of the 'situations' in which moral judgments are made.

CHAPTER FOUR

MORAL RULES AND MORAL JUDGMENT

A MORAL rule is a directive for right conduct to the effect that an act of a given kind x ought to be done on an occasion to which it is applicable. Thus a rule is by definition *general*, though rules may differ in their scope as to the numbers of people and the numbers of situations to which they are claimed to apply. Thus we could have:

1. Universal rules: *everyone* should do acts of kind x on *all* occasions. x here obviously cannot specify a class of acts such as telling the truth, since there may be occasions when one is not telling anybody anything. If there are such universal rules, they would therefore be general policy rules, e.g. one should always act from goodwill.
2. Rules universally specifying kinds of acts which everyone should do where the occasion arises: e.g. everyone ought to tell the truth when making statements conveying information.
3. Rules embodying qualifications to more general rules: everyone ought to tell the truth except on occasions of the kinds a, b, c . . . (e.g. where there might be danger to another person's life).
4. Rules applicable in a given society; in ancient Israel one should marry one's deceased brother's wife.

Rules of these kinds I shall call 'regulative': they give guidance for specific kinds of acts. There are two kinds of questions which arise over their universality: (*a*) questions about whether there can be a unique or preferred set of such rules, or whether there are a number of sets, acceptable according to different cultures; and (*b*) questions whether even within the rules of a particular culture there are rules prescribing how *all* men should behave or be treated, as well as rules prescribing the specific obligations which certain kinds of people have to certain other kinds of people (e.g. parents to children). The problems which cluster round (*a*) will concern us in the next chapter, on 'Moral Relativism'; those arising out of (*b*) when we come to look at the scope and possible limitations of 'role morality'.

Here our concern is on a more abstract plane: are there, besides these varieties of 'regulative' rules, rules which (adopting a Kantian terminology, though not perhaps in a Kantian sense) can be called 'constitutive principles'? That is to say, are there principles involved in the possibility of making a moral judgment at all, no matter what the moral judgment prescribes or forbids? An analogous distinction has been pointed out by John Rawls, between the rules which define a practice, and rules which may be arrived at by generalizations from experience and which can be maxims for doing well particular acts within the practice.[1] The clearest case is a game; there are the rules which set up the game, and maxims indicating how to play it well. As an example of a rule defining a moral practice, Rawls

[1] 'Two Concepts of Rules', *Philosophical Review* (1955) vol. 64. S. Zink, in *The Concepts of Ethics* (London, 1962), pp. 173 ff., has criticized Rawls' distinction, on the grounds that the rules of morality are not definitive of a practice, but directives (Zink, like Moore, sees them as directives on how to achieve maximum good). I think that, from a social point of view, Zink fails to appreciate Rawls' point about how morality often has to work within an institutional framework, and also, from a logical point of view, it is not certain that there are not some rules constitutive of morality as well as rules indicating how to follow it well. Also Rawls is concerned with the possibility of distinguishing between a utilitarian justification for an institution and a non-utilitarian justification for particular acts done according to its rules.

cites promising as *ipso facto* the incurring of an obligation to do what is promised, and he cites punishment as an institutional practice defined by rules which the judges and others administer. The analogy with the rules of a game cannot, as we have already seen, be pressed too far. I think, too, that the logical point (as in the example of promising) and the constitutional point (as in the example of judicial punishment) need more distinction. The problem over punishment is not just that it is possible to argue that it implies deserts by definition and that it is an institutional practice administered under rules; it is a problem of combining the various purposes it is intended to serve. Rawls is concerned to show that while there may be a utilitarian justification for the institution of punishment as a whole, its administration in the particular case is justified by rules for doing justice. In fact, however, though, according to Common Law, a man should not be punished except where guilt has been established by due procedures, utilitarian as well as retributive considerations can and do enter into the kind of sentence given in a particular case.[1] Rawls, however, has undoubtedly brought out an important feature of morality in corporate life; some things can only be done through established institutions operated by rules so that one has to work within the pattern they prescribe. This is perhaps the main point in his distinction when applied to social morality; it need not mean that no breaking of a rule of an institutional practice could be justified, or even possible, unless we abolish the institution altogether. The rules of institutions, unlike the rules setting up a game, are seldom as tight-knit as this.[2] That is to say, in the case of institutions, we need to distinguish constitutional rules of

[1] See below, p. 119.

[2] Even in a game, it is possible to cheat and yet still be said to be playing. F. P. Ramsey remarks on the 'scholasticism' of saying it is impossible to break the rules of bridge. *The Foundations of Mathematics*, p. 269. I owe the reference to Max Black, *Theoria* (1958), p. 148.

procedure as well as constitutive rules defining their practices. Constitutional rules define procedures and powers within an institution, and there are generally secondary rules prescribing procedures by which these can be changed.

A constitutive rule in morality would be a necessary condition for a practice being a moral practice at all. One candidate for such a constitutive rule has been called by Mr. Hare and others 'Universalizability'.[1] It is the rule 'treat like cases alike, and different cases differently': or, more precisely, 'if it is right to treat A in a certain way, it is right also so to treat others who resemble A in the relevant respect'. It is claimed (e.g. by Mr. Hare) that this is a *formal* criterion, neutral as between any substantive moral principles whatever.

I shall examine this claim, with the particular interest of trying to see whether it is in fact completely neutral as between all substantive moral rules, or whether, even if it is formally compatible in some sense with any set of moral rules, it may nevertheless give a reason for preferring some sets to others. This may be relevant when we come to the vexed question of moral relativism; behind this is the still more difficult question of whether the criterion itself may be culture bound. Or rather, even if it is indeed a criterion of a certain form of moral judgment, is this the only form or even the dominant form in all cultures? So far, only a few people like Professors Ladd and Brandt have looked at other people's ethical systems with this sort of logical interest in mind. It is the kind of question on which collaborative work between philosophers and anthropologists is called for; what kinds of moral judgment do people make and are there any general *constitutive* principles on which they proceed? (I repeat that this is a different question from the more popular question of whether or not

[1] See his paper 'Universalizability' in *Proceedings of the Aristotelian Society*, 1954–55. Also *Freedom and Reason* (Oxford, 1963).

there are any universal *regulative* principles prescribing what is right and what is wrong to which everyone making moral judgments would subscribe.)

To ask whether there are constitutive principles of *moral* judgments does of course assume moral *judgments*. To speak of a judgment is to speak of something which can be made more and less wisely or correctly; it precludes a view which says 'it is only a matter of opinion', with the implication that any opinion has an equal claim to consideration with any other. It also precludes one which says 'It is all a matter of feeling', with the implication that there is no *problem* in coming to a decision about what one ought to do; though it does not necessarily preclude a view which says that feelings of approval or disapproval, turned disinterested, may be at the basis of moral judgments.[1]

Broadly, by a moral judgment I am meaning a judgment guiding decisions as to what we ought to do, where the 'ought' concerns (*a*) a particular action in a situation, and (*b*) generally, though not always, a question of how we should treat other people, and (*c*) sometimes also a considered policy as to how we should live. Moral judgments may be given as deductive inferences, but they are often in fact more problematic than this. Aristotle, who drew attention to the practical syllogism, was also very aware that particular situations were complex; that how general rules were applied to them was not always obvious, so that one had to rely heavily on the judgment of the wise man of moral experience; and concluded that sometimes we might even have to say that the right act was the fortunate act. For there are difficulties about subsuming particular instances under the general principles: there may be two minor premises, e.g. if your major premise is that you

---

[1] In what follows, I shall be drawing, with modifications, on a paper of mine, 'Universalizability and Moral Judgment', in the *Philosophical Quarterly*, vol. XIII (1963), with permission of the Editor.

should not murder your neighbour, the question can arise as to whether this enemy in war is to count as a neighbour, and whether killing in war is to count as murder. Hence the moral problem of pacifism. Also different principles may be applicable to the same situation, but one can only be carried out at the cost of the other, and a decision has to be made on priorities. So though a moral judgment may be supported by what Mill calls 'considerations determining the mind to accept it', it need not only depend on deductive inference, and it will be problematic and corrigible. Indeed, I want to say that, if we are to speak of *judgment*, a basic requirement is that 'What ought I to do?' is seen as constituting a *problem*; that there is a difference between 'What do you think we should do?' and 'How do you react to this proposal?', or even 'How do you feel about it?' And if there is judgment, there is reflection, making use of comparisons and distinctions. Thus if there are indeed acts of decision for which no supporting reasons whatever can be given, which are completely unique, these decisions would not, I think, properly be called the result of *judgments*. I doubt whether there are such completely unique decisions, though the Existentialist notion of the *acte gratuit* may be an attempt to present moral decisions like this. But I do not see how there can be judgment without some discrimination of features of the situation in which it is made. Certainly these may not yield *sufficient* reasons from which what one ought to do can be deduced. But if they yield even considerations to be taken into account, then the judgment surely proceeds by making comparisons and distinctions between this situation and others, i.e., it is not *merely* directed to a unique situation.

Behind the term 'Universalizability' lies an attempt to make a rigorous formal principle out of this vaguely stated requirement, that what has been done in one situation is relevant to what should be done in another.

'Universalizability', as we have seen, is said to be one

of the formal characteristics of a moral principle, in that it should be general, in the sense that if it is right to treat A in a certain way, it is right also so to treat others who resemble A.[1] Sidgwick put the essential point: 'It cannot be right for A to treat B in a manner in which it would be wrong for B to treat A, merely on the ground that they are two different individuals, and without there being any difference between the natures or circumstances of the two which can be stated as a reasonable ground for difference of treatment'.[2] The principle would be compatible with egoism if this were egoism to the effect that I hold the best policy is for everyone to look after Number One, for this allows me to say that another person also should look after his Number One, though of course I shall compete with him. It would not be compatible with the egoism which says 'I for myself and everyone else for me', unless this were defended on 'Superman' lines, that I am a superior person. But then, if this is to be a moral policy, I should have to allow that someone should be substituted for me if he were a still more superior person. The principle can also hold even in the extreme case where *per absurdum* a solipsist, who holds he is the only existent, might be making a moral judgment. For a solipsist might follow a considered policy of pursuing his own perfection, and he could judge that if this were best furthered by doing act x now, it would be likely also to be best furthered by an act like x on another occasion like this one, if such were to arise.

If Universalizability is to be a criterion, we can ask what it excludes. If it means 'treat like cases alike', what is obviously excluded is arbitrariness in the sense of inconsistency in the application of a principle. Any principle

---

[1] In what follows, I owe a good deal to Mr. Gellner's paper, 'Ethics and Logic', and to Mr. Hare's paper, 'Universalizability', both in *Proceedings of the Aristotelian Society*, 1954–55, though I do not fully agree with either of them.

[2] *The Methods of Ethics*, 2nd edition, p. 353 (7th edition, p. 380).

could be in, provided it were applied consistently. But consistency is a mark of rationality in applying any sort of principle whatever, so it cannot be a sufficient, though it may be a necessary, criterion for a *moral* one. Universalizability demands the exclusion of principles which include proper names in their reference. Proper names are here not only ordinary ones like John Smith, but also logically proper names, i.e. terms such as 'you' and 'this' whose reference differs systematically according to the person using them. So if I claim that *I* ought to have exceptional treatment I am saying something which cannot be universalizable unless I claim the treatment not just because I am I, but in virtue of some property (e.g. having been ill on the day of the examination) which I should be prepared to allow as a ground for similar treatment in the case of other people. A difficulty here is that one could go on making more and more detailed distinctions of properties, which may be rare but can yet be stated without bringing in proper names, and enunciating principles to fit these. And then how specific can one get in distinguishing properties as principle-producing, i.e. saying that anyone with this property should be treated or should act in a certain way, without putting in so many detailed qualifications that one ends by describing the unique situation? If there were to be a unique rule for each unique occasion it would not count as a rule at all. As Wittgenstein said,[1] 'It is not possible that there should have been only one occasion on which someone obeyed a rule'. Or at any rate, he should be prepared for the rule to be obeyed on a subsequent occasion; rules may be made on one occasion and allowed to be precedent forming. If one were to counter the Kantian question 'Would you think it right for anyone else to do this in such a situation?' by saying that there will never be anyone else *just* like me, or a situation *just* like this, then we might get something like the Existentialist's unique act.

[1] *Philosophical Investigations* (Oxford, Blackwell, 1953), I, § 199.

But in that case we should have no basis for comparison or distinction, so we cannot be said to have a principle or a judgment as distinct from merely a decision about which nothing general can be said. That is to say, however detailed and spun-out our description of principle-producing properties, it has to stop short of a complete specification of the unique situation in terms none of which could be used of any other situation, if there is to be *judgment* as distinct from personal reaction.

Since the generality necessary for the Universalizability criterion is satisfied provided the principle invoked in the judgment does not contain proper names, it would be satisfied by saying, for instance, 'This is what I ought to do because this is how a Roman father ought to behave in this kind of situation'. We need not have to say 'this is how *any*one ought to behave'. Thus Universalizability would be compatible with moral relativism, in so far as conformity to very different role behaviour in different societies would satisfy the criterion. 'Roman father' is here taken as a class name, not a proper name. Tribal moralities can be brought within the Universalizability criterion if they are saying, not that 'This is how I, Brutus, should behave', but 'This is how all Roman fathers should behave in this sort of situation', also allowing, if pressed, a more general proposition, to the effect either that all fathers should behave like this, or that all fathers, whether Roman or not, should behave in the ways prescribed by their own *mores*.[1] Indeed, Universalizability so stated appears to fit relativism only too well; any principle, it would seem, can be in provided it is applied consistently. So there might be a formal universal character of moral principles combined with a substantive morality of rigid conformity to the local *mores*.

---

[1] Prof. Duncan Jones rules out 'tribal moralities' as morality on the score of particularity. But I do not think, with the provisos I have stated, this need be done. See *Butler's Moral Philosophy* (Pelican Books, 1952), p. 173.

In fact, to ask what are the conventions of the local *mores*, might be said to be a way of deciding between principles, if the Universalizability criterion itself provides no reason for preferring any one to another, and if any property whatsoever may be selected as the basis for a distinction on which a principle may be based.

In application, however, this arbitrariness is avoided because the Universalizability criterion gets conjoined with a notion of *relevant* likenesses and differences. 'Treat like cases alike, and different cases differently' is interpreted to mean 'Treat relevantly like cases alike, and relevantly different cases differently'.[1] But if a notion of relevance is built into Universalizability, then it is not being used as a purely formal criterion or, at any rate in use, it has to be conjoined with a decision on a non-formal point. For though it may be possible to give a general definition of relevance, e.g. 'material to the point at issue', in order to decide whether a distinction is relevant or not, we must know what the point at issue is. If there is not a built-in appeal to relevance, *any* distinguishing property can be made into a basis for a principle allowing for differential treatment to those possessing it. Thus, suppose I say, 'All black men

[1] See, e.g., R. M. Hare, *Proceedings of the Aristotelian Society*, 1954–55, p. 299. A patriot should think that other people owe similar duties to their countries 'unless he points to *relevant* differences between his country and others'. In a discussion of the 'Ideal Observer' theory, which I shall suggest involves a form of Universalizability from the point of view of a spectator, Professor Firth says the Ideal Observer must react alike to acts which are the same in 'ethically relevant respects'. He admits a qualm about whether this phrase can be defined without circularity; and if the test of an ethically relevant respect is that it is one to which an Ideal Observer reacts in a certain way, I hardly see how this can fail to be circular. Professor Brandt, who continues the discussion, does not even have qualms. He talks *passim* of 'morally relevant differences' in situations, and of 'morally relevant properties' as those to be selected for universalizable reactions.

should be paid more than all white men'. True, I must exclude logical proper names, and say that I should be prepared myself to be paid less as a white man. And with this *proviso* it could be said this principle conforms to the Universalizability criterion. Let us take a more bizarre example: 'All persons with pimples on their noses ought to be promoted in their jobs'. Most of us would want to say that whether or not you have a pimple on your nose is irrelevant to whether you are suitable for promotion; that it does not make sense to say that people having just any similar distinguishing property should be treated alike, but that the distinguishing property should be one relevant to the treatment. Therefore, in actual application Universalizability is used in conjunction with this non-formal notion of relevance, to attack or defend differential treatment as given to different kinds of people. It says 'treat alike people who have a relevantly resembling property and differently people who have another relevant property'.

Professor M. G. Singer[1] has an admirable discussion of various kinds of moral argument of the form: 'If it is right, or wrong, for one person to do a thing, then it would be right or wrong for everyone to do it', and also discusses the characteristics of justifiable and unjustifiable claims that an exception should be made to a general rule. Singer shows that if the *reason* cited for the exception is one for which any other reason could equally well be substituted, or which could equally apply to anyone whomsoever, then anyone could just as well be an exception as anyone else, and so no valid reason has been given. Thus, if someone argues that he need not pay his taxes not because he has a special reason for exemption, but because the government will not miss his contribution, this consideration could apply to anyone, and so make anyone claim he could be an exception. The sense in which Universalizability as a general principle is compatible with admitting exceptions

[1] In *Generalization in Ethics* (London, 1963).

to specific rules lies in maintaining that no one ought to claim to be an exception if there is no reason why he should be. In this way, Universalizability could be a general constitutive principle, which would hold in all circumstances, whereas particular 'regulative' moral rules may admit of exceptions.

A similar distinction must be made in interpreting the famous 'Golden Rule' which appears in a number of cultures: 'Do unto others as you would have them do unto you', or, in its negative form, 'Do not unto others as you would not have them do unto you'. Bernard Shaw once made the quip that you should not do to others what you would have them do to you, because tastes differ. He is perfectly correct if the Golden Rule is taken to mean: 'Do to other people the particular things you would have done to you, and don't do to them the particular things you would not have done to you'. This could commit me to giving a teenage god-daughter philosophy books and not pop records for a Christmas present. But if we stress the *as* in 'Do to others *as* . . .', and do not say *what*, the Golden Rule becomes the general constitutive rule 'Act on the same principles and standards to other people as you would have them act towards you'.[1] This will mean taking account of relevant differences.

Can anything more be said in general about this notion of relevance of reasons for differential treatment? I shall call relevance a 'right-conferring reason' for a judgment. And a right I shall call, borrowing Professor Hart's term, a 'defeasible' concept.[2] That is to say, it stakes out a claim as valid, and the claim may be challenged. And if the challenge cannot be met, the right will be not only defeasible, but defeated. So it will not be enough to say that 'All

[1] On this, cf. M. G. Singer, 'The Golden Rule', *Philosophy*, vol. XXXVIII, Oct. 1963.

[2] 'The Ascription of Responsibility and Rights', *Proceedings of the Aristotelian Society* (1948–49), N.S. vol. XLIX, pp. 171 ff.

black men ought to be paid more than all white men' can be a moral principle provided I would apply it also to myself.[1] One must be able to defend distinction in colour as a 'right-conferring' reason for differential treatment. And this can start an argument, turning perhaps on questions of fact, perhaps on an ideological belief put forward as though it were a question of fact (e.g. belief in inherent racial superiority); or perhaps on a traditional religious story cited as giving authority. These arguments will be put forward as *legitimatizing reasons*; some of them may be bizarre, and they may include factual beliefs which can be true or false. But once they are put forward, they can be challenged, for instance by people with more accurate knowledge of the facts. Thus they become problematic, and the door is opened to further argument, for, since relevance is not a purely formal notion, it has to be defended by appeal to substantive considerations. Its point is to exclude arbitrariness not only in the application of a principle, but in the property selected as a basis in drawing it up.

It might be said that in this last phrase 'basis' suggests that a fact about a property entails a principle about an obligation. We do in practice cite factual propositions in support of arguments about what we ought to do, but in the total argument (or more likely its presuppositions) some of these factual propositions are likely to be value laden through more basic principles, or through policies for living. Sometimes also the factual part of the argument will serve to show an inconsistency with the factual part of an opponent's argument, or other factual parts of one's own. Thus one may start from assuming in accordance with traditional *mores* that prisoners taken in war can be made into slaves.

---

[1] Mr. Hare (*Freedom and Reason*, Ch. IX) says that if one says this, one is logically impeccable in making a moral judgment; one can only be vulnerable to an argument about the function of morality, as concerned, e.g., with considering people's interests.

But once begin arguing about moral reasons (as distinct from mere reasons of power) why someone may be made a slave, and one may find oneself having to argue, as Aristotle did, that the man who is to be a slave is not capable of making rational decisions (here there is a basic major premise that no one capable of rational decisions ought to be made a slave), and then, how does this apply to prisoners of war; and finally how does it apply to anyone? (This question was very properly raised by some of the Sophists.) Thus, argument on facts makes one uncover one's more basic principles and the ways in which factual premises get subsumed under them as minor premises, and this may help to show up unplausibility. So in our example, 'All persons with pimples on their noses ought to be promoted in their jobs', we might try to legitimatize this by a more general principle that people who work hard ought to be promoted; and people who work hard have no time for exercise and get pimples. . . . And by this time the shakiness of the logic will be apparent as well as the questionable nature of the factual statement. At any rate, the argument gets started, and the legitimatizing claims may not only be defeasible, but defeated.

If, however, we say that not only inconsistency in the application of principles but also arbitrariness in the selection of properties named in them is excluded, then Universalizability, as it operates in actual moral judgments, does not just use the formal criterion of consistency, nor is it sufficient merely to say that it excludes proper names. To exclude arbitrariness, the property cited as a justifying reason for a decision must be defended as relevant. Then the point about Universalizability will be that a moral judgment should be regarded *either as appealing to precedent or as precedent-forming*. In claiming the right to give someone differential treatment, one should either appeal to a precedent, or be prepared for one's action to form one. So where a proper name is cited in a particular case and, for instance,

I am prepared to allow John Smith to have a special examination, I must be prepared to argue relevant supporting reasons, and to allow my decision to form a precedent if another case arises where similar supporting reasons can be cited. In Manchester applications for a special examination go to an Applications Committee of Senate which is a sort of court of equity, and a reason has to be given 'satisfactory to Senate'. In a recent application (which was allowed) a candidate said that he had been unable to get to the examination because an elephant had been sitting on the line in the path of his train. The need to argue *relevant* supporting reasons for the action will be the answer to the suggestion that, on Universalizability alone, *any* unlikely concatenation of circumstances can be stated in general terms so as to be maxim-producing. The unlikely concatenation of circumstances is seen as one to which a principle is applicable. The maxim is not just 'All candidates prevented from attendance by elephants sitting on the railway line shall be allowed a special examination'. It is 'All candidates prevented by obstacles not of their own fault . . .' But the particular case provides a precedent whereby if in a future case an elephant on the line is pleaded as such an obstacle it must be allowed to count.[1]

Thus the notion of Universalizability operates within a context where a judicial spirit is assumed; this consists in making impartial judgments, in arguing distinctions between relevant and irrelevant reasons for differential treatment, in appealing to precedents and in realizing that new decisions must be allowed to form precedents which can be used to establish new principles. It thus calls for qualities which

[1] Is this Kant's point, when he says that one must be able to *will* that the maxim of one's action should be a universal law? And this is not the same as saying, as Kant is sometimes represented as saying, that we can deduce substantive principles from the test of consistency alone. I owe this suggested analogy with a way of interpreting Kant to a conversation with Professor Körner.

will be more likely to be forthcoming in systems which have such a notion of judicial impartiality. So even if it be abstractly compatible with any system whatsoever, in practice it provides a reason for preferring such systems as inculcate the qualities necessary for its own application.

I now pass to another suggested criterion of judgments as moral judgments: that they are directed to actions towards which approbation and disapprobation are felt. Formally, this is compatible with approbation or disapprobation towards anything whatever, provided these are felt consistently. I must not say I approve of *you* doing this (e.g. taking a day off work), but would not approve of anyone else doing it, unless I can argue differential reasons for approving of your doing it which I should allow in other cases. Consistency in approbation and disapprobation may indeed be said to be Universalizability applied from the point of view of a spectator of an action passing judgment on it, as distinct from an agent considering what he ought to do. The agent can of course pass judgment on his own actions. Consistency in judgment directed also to oneself is the 'disinterestedness' of Adam Smith's 'impartial spectator'. Westermarck held that disinterested sympathetic and reprobatory sentiments are the roots of morality (i.e. sentiments which can be dissociated from one's personal interests and preferences). Whether or not they are 'roots' in the sense of the controversial empirical question of *origins*, a good case can be made for making their disinterestedness part of the definition of moral emotions. Westermarck writes: 'When pronouncing an act good or bad, I mean that it is so quite independently of any reference it might have to me personally', and 'Resentment and retributive kindly emotion are moral emotions if they are assumed by those who feel them to be uninfluenced by the particular relationship in which they stand both to those who are immediately affected by the acts in question and

F

those who perform the acts'.[1] It is noteworthy that Wester-marck gave the title of *Ethical Relativity* to the book in which he summarized this view, put forward at length in *The Origin and Development of the Moral Sentiments*. He was concerned to illustrate the diversity of *mores*, but at the same time thought this was compatible with a criterion of disinterestedness as marking the distinction between senti-ments of personal resentment and moral sentiments.

Note that I have switched from talking about moral judgments to talking about moral sentiments. But I think that to speak of 'disinterested' approbation or disapproba-tion is to speak of how a sentiment can have some of the characteristics of a judgment. A sentiment may be 'sub-jective', in that there must be a subject to feel it, and a proper name is used in expressing it. Thus 'Honesty is approved of by me' is a statement or proposition about my approval of honesty, but 'I approve of honesty' is an expression of my approval. But the expression, though subjective as put in the first person, is not merely subjective in the self-centred sense if it expresses a consistent attitude to all acts of honesty whether they affect my interests or not, and whether I or someone else does them (perhaps to my disadvantage). That is, the *objects* of the attitudes do not depend on the inclusion of proper names. This trans-poses the Universalizability criterion to an attitude, and thereby endows the attitude with a characteristic of rational judgment. Nevertheless I think there is a difference, in that in moral judgments properties of persons and situations are specified as bases for principles for similar or differential treatment, whereas an attitude need not be articulated by maxims using common nouns. It may be more like a total assertion (to use a term of the late Professor J. L. Stocks),[2] a response to the action as a whole ('I approve of this'), and

[1] *Ethical Relativity* (London, 1932), pp. 90, 93.
[2] See *Reason and Intuition and Other Essays*, edited by Dorothy Emmet (London, 1939), p. 38.

therefore may be the more appropriate idiom for evaluating the particular unique action in a particular situation. But of course when reasons are sought for the evaluation, then the logical proper name 'this' only appears as indicating that we have an instance of an act of a given kind.

Professors Firth and Brandt have developed this 'rational attitude' view further, so as also to eliminate the logical proper name 'I' of the holder of the attitude, by a theory of an 'Ideal Observer' as the referent of moral reactions.[1] The Ideal Observer is a reincarnation in a more precisely delineated form of Adam Smith's 'Impartial Spectator'. An Ideal Observer is defined by Professor Firth as one who would know all the facts, could visualize the consequences of all possible alternative actions, and was impartial, in the sense of not being influenced by particular interests (viz. those needing proper names for their designation). It is easy to point out that an Ideal Observer who knew all the facts and the consequences of all possible alternatives and was completely impartial could only be God. Firth indeed says the Ideal Observer need not exist: we only need to be able to say, 'This is how such a one would react'. If this is not only intended as a theoretical definition of what it would be for an act to be right (i.e. it would be one of which such an Ideal Observer would approve), but is also meant as a criterion in practice, how do we work it, since patently we cannot ourselves fulfil these requisites, or even know how someone having them would react? Professor Brandt tries to bring the Ideal Observer down to earth, and make him more human and normal, and even a possible empirical character. He need not be omniscient, but merely be required to believe correctly all facts which would make a difference to his reaction; and be impartial in that his

[1] Cf. *Philosophy and Phenomenological Research* (1951–52), vol. XII and (1954–55), vol. XV, no. 3; and, for Professor Brandt's view, also his books *Hopi Ethics* (Chicago, 1954) and *Ethical Theory* (New York, 1959).

reactions must be the same in all situations where people have the same relevant properties. Brandt thinks it is possible to think of an actual empirical observer fulfilling these requirements. He must be 'qualified', defined as sane, possessed of correct beliefs on the relevant facts in a maximally clear and vivid form, not be ill, not in a condition of physical craving, fatigued, excited, nor depressed, and have a strong and favourable sentiment towards all human beings and no biassing towards particular groups or statuses.[1] We may comment that this is a large order. How can we be sure that anyone possesses correct beliefs on the facts (as well as knowing what facts are relevant) in a *maximally* clear and vivid form? Brandt indeed acknowledges that this may be an ideal, comparable to a frictionless plane. But then we are back with the *Ideal* Observer, and away from 'human and normal' observers with qualified attitudes. We can say that observers with qualified attitudes are those that approximate to this ideal. But if there is no empirical test that they have it in an absolute sense (and how indeed could there be?), then it is always possible that two observers who differ in their reactions are not equally qualified according to some of Brandt's requirements.

Nevertheless, the Ideal Observer theory is of special interest for our purpose because, in transposing to the point of view of a spectator the qualities which an agent needs if he is to think in terms of Universalizability, it brings out the non-formal aspects of this criterion. It does this by delineating in some detail an ideal of judicial impartiality. And if this ideal of judicial impartiality characterizes the attitude of Ideal Observers, I suggest they cannot be completely neutral as between different moral systems, but will have a reason to prefer those moral systems which encourage this attitude. Thus an appeal to Ideal Observers would set some limitation on complete ethical relativity.

[1] *Hopi Ethics*, pp. 239–240.

At least, it would do so if it is right to say that all Ideal Observers should have the attitude of judicial impartiality. And here we have to consider the possibility that this ideal itself may be 'culture bound', in that some systems of judicial morality look on the prime requisite in a judge as not impartiality, but skill in suggesting workable ways of harmonizing conflicting interests.[1] It is said, moreover, that some peoples (e.g. the Pueblo Indians) would find particularly odd our view that it is the 'disinterested spectator', non-kin, non-involved, who is best fitted to pass critical moral judgments. They would say that it was none of his business. The people qualified to judge are one's own kin or people to whom one stands in some special relationship.[2] And, more important for our argument, it might also be claimed that sometimes Ideal Observers might have more trustworthy reactions when not in an attitude of judicial impartiality, but when they are deeply sympathetic to one of the parties, or even in a towering rage. Mr. Jonathan Harrison suggests this rather mildly in his contribution to the discussion,[3] when he queries whether an Ideal Observer should be dispassionate, and says that the 'sympathy' of Adam Smith's Impartial Spectator was a 'passion'. Adam Smith in fact calls sympathy a 'fellow feeling with any passion of another whatsoever'. But his point is similar to that of the advocates of the Universalizability criterion; we must be able to pass judgment on our own conduct as we would on that of another person and

[1] See J. Ladd, *The Structure of a Moral Code*, pp. 70 ff. To see that other interests besides mine ought to be taken into account is, however, a feature coming within the purview of the Universalizability criterion (i.e. *interests* as such must be regarded, and not only those with the logically proper possessive pronoun 'my').

[2] See M. and A. Edel, *Anthropology and Ethics*, p. 100 (American Lecture Series, Springfield, Ill.). It would be good to have more field evidence on this.

[3] *Philosophy and Phenomenological Research* (1956–57), vol. XVII, pp. 25 ff.

vice versa. 'We endeavour to examine our own conduct as we imagine any other fair and impartial spectator would examine it. If, upon placing ourselves in his situation, we thoroughly enter into all the passions and motives which influenced it, we approve of it, by sympathy with the approbation of this supposed equitable judge. If otherwise, we enter into his disapprobation and condemn it.'[1] Sympathy can therefore go along with the capacity to put oneself imaginatively into the role of the impartial spectator. It means not the same as approval, but the capacity to feel passions and motives while at the same time looking at them with the detachment proper to this new role.

This is to say that the notion of being 'free from passion' is ambiguous: it may mean 'without passion' or 'detached from passion'. Professor Brandt might indeed reply to Harrison that his Ideal Observer is not just a cold fish; he is to have 'a strong and favourable sentiment towards all human beings', and this, as affective goodwill, can be distinguished from the kind of sympathy which is an emotion inclining one to favour a particular person. Yet if we see someone hurt, there may be sympathy with him as hurt, and this sympathy can give rise to an emotion inclining one to favour him, but also to a concern to understand the situation in which he was hurt. If (say) this was a fight, should the sympathy by itself decide how we judge its rights and wrongs? Similarly with the angry Ideal Observer. In other words, an Ideal Observer might judge better if he were sympathetic, angry, or even excited, since these emotions might arouse and sustain his concern. But nevertheless, I think we should hold that he should have 'freedom of spirit' in being able to detach these emotions from his personal preferences and interests. It may be possible to feel disinterested approbation and disapprobation in a hot as well as in a cold form.

If this is so, the ideal of impartiality *can* be said to hold a

[1] *The Theory of Moral Sentiments*, part III, § i.

privileged place among moral ideals. And it can be said to occupy the peculiar position of being both a substantive virtue and also part of the form of moral judgments. Professor D. H. Monro has questioned this in an article, 'Impartiality and Consistency',[1] saying that those who appeal to Universalizability confuse, or conflate, the logical principle of consistency with the moral principle of impartiality, and while consistency is a formal principle for applying all principles, and not only moral ones, impartiality is a substantive virtue. So to say 'One ought to make exceptions in one's own favour' is not to *fail* to make a moral judgment (as it would be were impartiality a formal criterion), but to make a particular judgment, which most people would say was an immoral one, and which at any rate could be significantly denied. I come very near to agreeing with this, since I have been concerned to show that Universalizability is not only a neutral and formal criterion. But while Professor Monro wishes to distinguish Universalizability as consistency from impartiality, I think that the main proponents of Universalizability as a criterion (for instance, Mr. Hare) are right in seeing that consistency in moral judgment calls for impartiality in the application of a principle, and this means applying it to oneself. So 'One ought not to make exceptions in one's own favour' *does* seem to follow from consistency in moral judgment. And yet at the same time impartiality is *also* a substantive moral principle. I think that the implication of this is that the criterion of logical consistency when applied in morals is not only rational but also *fair*.

In *Freedom and Reason* Mr. Hare carries further the view that Universalizability is consistency in applying a principle wherever the descriptive meaning of the terms applicable in one situation is the same as it is in another situation. To take a non-ethical example, if I call a thing red I am committed to calling anything else just like it red too. Hare claims that this is no more than a formal point of logic.

[1] *Philosophy* (April–July 1961), vol. XXXVI.

Qua consistency it is neutral as between substantive principles, but *qua* impartiality in applying moral ones, I maintain that we can defend allowing what counts as a reason in one case to count in a similar case as not only consistent but as also as *fair*, and its violation as unfair. Perhaps we should say that the *prescriptive* force in saying that *moral* principles should be universalizable includes a conviction that this is not only rational but fair. If so, justice, not in the sense of particular rules, but in the very general sense of equitable fairness, does seem to have a special place among moral notions.

There are, then, two respects in which Universalizability draws on non-formal notions in its operation. The first is the appeal to relevance, in order to distinguish properties in virtue of which principles are applied. There may of course be cases where a decision is made intuitively, without one's being able to cite reasons, i.e. to say in virtue of what features of the situation some principle may be said to apply. This is analogous to those administrative situations in which an application is granted, with the rider 'that it should not form a precedent'. If such a decision is more than just a surrender to sentiment, it probably expresses an intuitive conviction that this is the right decision and that it is not likely to have repercussions in this case, though we should not know how to justify it as a general practice. If it were possible to justify it explicitly, this would be 'in virtue of' certain characteristics of the situation, i.e. Universalizability would be being invoked. The Existentialists may be calling attention to the fact that there are sometimes such intuitive decisions (or reactions) on moral problems. The 'Universalizabilists' (to coin a horror term) may be calling attention to the fact that if justificatory grounds are cited for a decision, and if these are to be rational, they will be cited in terms which imply comparisons and distinctions, i.e. which do not refer uniquely to this one situation. Some Existentialists may of course say that moral decisions can have no justificatory grounds. Perhaps *aesthetic* judgments may be immediate and intuitive, unsupported by grounds or principles. But is it a difference between a moral and an aesthetic judgment that it matters whether a moral judgment is *fair*? Or, if in a particular case we decide not to try to be fair in the equalitarian sense, as in giving a handicapped child a larger share of something, there should be a reason for this which can be defended in an equitable sense; and so, again, we see that the judgment, if it is to be a moral judgment, draws on considerations not just unique to the particular case, and not just citing personal preferences. Thus the non-formal notion we are using is fairness; or rather, we are claiming that consistency in the application of moral rules takes on the substantive moral character of fairness. Equity, indeed, as an attempt to take account of special circumstances, where the rigid application of rules could produce an anomaly, is itself guided by a will to do justice, as Aristotle saw.[1] And notoriously, Equity itself turns into a kind of law.

All this looks like an apologia for liberal morality. Maybe it is; but if so, I have tried to base the defence on an argument that this kind of morality allows for the development of moral judgment itself through inculcating a property of fairness necessary for its application. I have not tried to argue that its principles are rationally self-evident, or generally accepted in some form or another, or have divine backing.

The argument is thus not an argument against moral relativism in favour of a single universal code. Nor is it a 'natural law' argument in the ordinary sense, which tries to find evidence for a generally accepted and acceptable universal code. The conclusion, however, bears some resemblance to the notion of 'natural justice' as it appears in the English Common Law.[2] 'Natural justice' is here not

[1] *Nicomachean Ethics*, V, x.

[2] I have a certain pleasure in pointing out this analogy; the first philosophical paper I published, a good many years ago in *Philosophy*

a shorthand expression for a code of absolute principles. It defines certain rules of procedure by following which it is held that just verdicts are more likely to be reached: viz. that no man should be judge in his own case; that anyone accused should know what he is accused of; and that he should be able to make his defence. The emphasis is thus on a process which is deemed to make fair and reasonable decisions more likely. The analogy with the Common Law can be pressed further in respect of the use of precedent. In Common Law decisions on cases are used to establish principles to be followed in succeeding cases (*stare decisis*). American Law is less precedent-bound than English Law; in English Law emphasis is put on the need for at least an appearance of *certainty* in the law through reference to precedents. But there is also the recognition (though it may work slowly and creakingly) that simply to follow precedent may serve to perpetuate error, if there is reason to question the principle extracted from the precedent-forming decision. So the doctrine *communis error facit ius* can be challenged. Higher courts can overrule precedents established in inferior courts. Till July 1966 it was generally accepted that the highest court of the land, the House of Lords, was bound by its own previous decisions. Here therefore a precedent could only be challenged by distinguishing points of fact so that it could be argued not to apply, or by waiting for a change in the law through Act of Parliament. But Lord Justice Denning has recently pointed out[1] that even the House of Lords has not been so bound over the whole of our legal history; and he enters a plea that it

(1939), vol. XIV, was one on 'Justice and Equality' in which I tried to show the difference between the English Common Law notion of Natural Justice as prescribing rules of judicial procedure, and the traditional Natural Law theory of a single universal rational moral code. And now I find myself returning to this distinction.

[1] 'From Precedent to Precedent' (Romanes Lecture, Oxford, 1959).

should be bolder on occasion in going behind its own precedents. There is also an interesting statement by Lord
Justice Goddard, in allowing the appeal in Rex v. Taylor [1]
where he urges that the Court of Criminal Appeal should
reconsider its own interpretation of the law as given in a
previous decision. 'A court of appeal in civil matters usually
considers itself bound by its own decisions or by decisions
of a court of co-ordinate jurisdiction. For instance, it considers itself bound by its own decisions and those of the
Exchequer Chamber; and as is well known the House of
Lords also always considers itself bound by its own decisions. In civil matters this is essential in order to preserve
the rule of *stare decisis*.

'This court, however, has to deal with questions involving the liberty of the subject, and if it finds on reconsidera-
tion that, in the opinion of a full court, assembled for that
purpose, the law has been either misapplied or misunderstood in a decision which it has previously given, and that,
on the strength of that decision, an accused person has been
sentenced and imprisoned, it is the bounden duty of the
court to reconsider the earlier decision with a view to seeing
whether that person had been properly convicted.'

In morality, unlike law, there is no recognized procedure
by which the finality of a precedent can be challenged either
by appeal or by changing the law through Act of Parliament. Yet there is an analogy, though the appeal is not
to the policy of the statute, but to a contemporary sense of
what is fair and reasonable. (I suspect that in the breaking of a precedent in law, these are in fact closely connected, though the latter in English Law at least must get
expressed in terms of the former.) When a *decision is made*
as a moral judgment, we must indeed be prepared for the
maxim expressing its ground to be precedent-forming for
future cases. But this maxim can *later* come to be subject

[1] Rex v. Taylor, (1950) 2 K.B. pp. 368–371. I owe the reference
to H. L. A. Hart, *The Concept of Law* (Oxford, 1961), p. 150.

to revision and criticism through the sense of what constitutes a fair decision, otherwise any maxim, however perverse, would have to be perpetuated in the name of Universalizability. This criticism again may be corrigible; the arguments for a moral judgment are, I have said, open-ended.

If, then, Universalizability can in fact be shown to be a criterion of moral judgments and if it has to be worked by a judicial sense for what constitutes fair decisions, it looks as though, however varied the notions may be of what constitutes justice materially, the will to do justice has more than an accidental connection with moral judgments, because it serves not only as a guide in the process of making and applying them, but also by being one ingredient at any rate in whatever purpose or purposes they serve.

'Whatever purpose or purposes they serve.' This, broadly, suggests an *ethical theory* about the function of morality, and the character of its claims. I do not see that this can be avoided; nor do I see any ethical theory uncontroversially accepted by all moral philosophers, let alone everyone else. We must then, I believe, accept the fact that there is more than one possible type of ethical theory, and be prepared to argue for which seems to us the most plausible. For this reason, there is another form of the alleged 'autonomy of ethics' which I do not think can be sustained. This is the view that there can be a second-order study, meta-ethics, a study of the language of morals, which is neutral not only as between different substantive first-order moral views (i.e. normative views about what is right and what is wrong), but also as between ethical theories, such as ethics of pure principle, or Utilitarian ethics, or 'attitude' theories. I do not think this is possible, because, as I have already remarked, there is no self-evident or agreed ethical terminology. A sharp separation of a first- and second-order study may be possible where this condition is fulfilled, or where we can work within stipulated definitions, perhaps, for instance, in branches of mathematics, but not where the whole subject is problematic. In ethics, the central notions, 'right', 'good', 'duty', 'obligation', 'responsibility', to name only a few, are used with differing emphasis and are differently related to each other in the kinds of first-order moral judgments which people make. Hence anyone who sets out to discuss the meaning of ethical terms will be bound to produce an ethical theory, which can be controverted. Examples are Professor Nowell Smith's *Ethics*[1] and Mr. Hare's *The Language of Morals*,[2] each of which while starting out as a logical-linguistic study, in fact develops an ethical theory, Professor Nowell Smith's in terms of human ends and interests, Mr. Hare's in terms of rationality and sincerity in the application of principles. Thus, according to the theory held, there will be different views of the character of moral argument, and of the ways in which ethical terms are related, and which of them is fundamental.[3] So 'meta-ethics' in effect calls for decisions about what is held to be the function of ethics. These are of course decisions of a general theoretical kind. It might still be contended that they are independent of any particular substantive views about right and wrong in any positive *mores*. But we saw that positive *mores* are not always accepted unquestioningly; that people can ask for reasons why they prescribe and proscribe what they do. These reasons may be tilted towards one type of ethical theory rather than another. If they go in a Utilitarian direction, facts about possible consequences will become relevant in a way in which they may not if the argument goes in the direction of trying to show that certain

[1] Pelican Books, 1954. [2] Oxford, 1952.

[3] Mr. A. W. H. Adkins has produced a study of Greek Ethics called *Merit and Responsibility* (Oxford, 1960), the burden of which is to show that the early Greeks did *not* have a notion of responsibility. Such a book could hardly have been written by someone who did not think responsibility was an important ethical notion.

principles are intuitively right, or right in virtue of accepted religious authority. What is a good reason for a moral belief in one type may not be a good reason in another, so differences in the type of ethical theory held may indeed come to affect people's substantive judgments of what they think right and wrong.

I conclude that a completely neutral and morally aseptic 'meta-ethics' is not practicable.[1] This does not mean that ethics cannot be treated by different approaches, descriptively, normatively, logically[2] and on different levels of generality. But since ethics is problematic at every level, the first-order substantive judgments of right and wrong cannot just remain unaffected by discussions on the more theoretical levels, as they might if these were firmer and less controversial than is in fact the case. Similarly, the kind of ethical theory one holds is not likely to be unaffected by one's actual moral convictions, for instance by how seriously one takes morality as *personal* and how seriously as *social*, or whether one tries to see how it can be both of these.

If one fastens on the aspect of morality as social, within an institutional setting, I have little doubt that the most plausible theory is the one called 'Rule Utilitarianism'.[3] This recognizes that moral conduct is on the whole rule guided. We do not think out afresh in each situation whether we should, e.g., commit a theft, or a murder, or

[1] Cf. A. Gewirth, 'Meta-Ethics and Normative Ethics', *Mind* (April, 1960), N.S. LXIX. I am in close agreement with this interesting article.

[2] 'Deontic Logic' is an attempt to set up deductive formal systems with rules in which ethical concepts enter through definitions. It is not a discussion of the problematic meaning of ethical terms, the most plausible ways of relating them, and the claims to knowledge which may be being made in their use. My concern with the 'logic of ethics' is in this latter older-fashioned sense of 'logic'.

[3] For a close exposition, cf. R. Brandt, *Ethical Theory* (Prentice Hall Philosophy Series, 1959), pp. 39 ff. See also R. M. Hare, *Freedom and Reason*, pp. 130 ff.

whether or not we should tell the truth. Yet rules are not left in the air without justification, or justified simply by custom or self-evident intuition. They are said to be justified because they prescribe the kind of conduct which is likely on the whole to promote the interests and happiness of people living together in a society. Thus it is not necessary, as in 'act Utilitarianism', to ask in each instance what action is most likely to maximize happiness. Indeed, to take each case 'on its merits' would be very time-consuming, even if the sums could be realistically worked out.[1] Bentham may have thought this should be done; Mill on the whole was a 'rule' Utilitarian.[2] It is more feasible to ask the Utilitarian question about rules for practices, and to observe them unless there is some very good reason not to do so. On the 'rule Utilitarian' view the result of keeping to the practice in a particular case should be judged likely to be really disastrous in order to justify breaking it, since the desirability of not weakening observances which are for the general interest has to be taken into account before making an exception.[3] Rule Utilitarianism thus justifies acts indirectly, as being acts of a particular kind, and fits social morality well, both in showing the place of established rules and practices, and in looking for a justification of these in common interests. Its way of relating rules and ends can suit the conditions of social morality where what people's main interests are and what is likely to make for happiness is, if not agreed, at any rate a matter of public discussion. Some needs come to be generally accepted as

[1] A valiant attempt to live like this was made by 'Shoemaker Hankin' in L. P. Jacks' story called 'Mad Shepherds'.

[2] Cf. J. O. Urmson, *Philosophical Quarterly* (1953), vol. III, p. 33, 'The Interpretation of the Moral Philosophy of J. S. Mill'.

[3] G. E. Moore, who can be described as a rule Utilitarian concerned for the maximizing of good, was so impressed by this that he was reluctant to justify any exceptions. See his *Principia Ethica*, Chapter V.

reasonable claims, many being summed up under the term 'welfare'; and their discussion finds a context in terms of the dominant values of the way of life of the community.[1] Rule Utilitarianism is thus plausible as a theory of social and institutional morality within a broadly accepted context. Is it equally plausible as a theory of personal morality?

There is indeed one time-honoured form of personal morality, which looks at first as if it should be described as a high form of such Utilitarianism. Rules are given their place as prescribing conduct likely to be conducive to the achievement of a goal or 'purpose in life'. Such a teleological theory has its difficulties. There can be conflicts between the ends one thinks good to pursue, just as there can be conflicts between principles. Can these be resolved by saying that there can be one master end which one should pursue in all circumstances, and to which other lesser ends are subordinate? That there should be a *summum bonum* for the moral life of the individual has been the hope of a host of teleological moralists from Aristotle onwards. The trouble is that such an end, if it is to be sufficiently general to hold in all circumstances, tends to get stated in such nebulous terms that it ceases to be sufficiently specific for the 'means-end' calculation to be plausible. (How, in fact, does one define 'happiness' or 'beatitude', or 'glorifying God' — some of the main candidates for Man's Chief End?) On the other hand, if an overriding end is made so specific that it is plausible to say that a person might plan his whole life so as to pursue it (for instance, amassing a fortune, or becoming Prime Minister), it is to say the least dubious that such an end ought to be pursued at all costs and in all circumstances. Moreover, people vary in how far they unify their activities with a view to some master purpose. Those that do so most successfully are not necessarily those who are most sensitive to the claims and

[1] Cf. S. I. Benn, 'Interests in Politics', *Proceedings of The Aristotelian Society* (1960), N.S. vol. LX.

needs of other people. 'The *Summum Bonum*', said E. F. Carritt,[1] 'has, I believe, been the *ignis fatuus* of moral philosophy.' Even one who, like myself, is sympathetic to a teleological element in morality can see this elusiveness.

The phrases used to point to a 'Chief End' are, I think, better interpreted as expressing the orientation or policy [2] by which a person lives his life and approaches his moral decisions, rather than as an objective at which these decisions are aimed: e.g. the will to live in an 'agapeistic' way (Professor Braithwaite's phrase), or in a way that increases happiness, or expresses love to God. Such a dominant orientation is expressed through a person's acts; it is not naturally described in the language of means and ends appropriate to Utilitarianism. Moreover, in the morality of personal relations we are often not directly aware of rules, ends, interests. The dominant feature of such morality may be a general attitude of consideration for the other person; hence some people say that it simply depends upon 'love'. But love is not always wise unless a person is prepared to think, and sometimes think hard, about what he is doing; and to think is to become aware of questions about consequences, needs, purposes, other people's interests — which are also the matters of social morality. The distinction is not therefore a complete one; and still less so, since goodwill as well as reason can inform even the more impersonal social morality. In the morality of direct personal relations the emphasis on the expression of attitudes is indeed more marked, and it can pervade considerations of interests, needs, purposes and the like. Nevertheless these are the sort of considerations which form the subject

---

[1] *The Theory of Morals* (Oxford, 1928), p. 74.

[2] The term 'policy' has been used in this connection by R. B. Braithwaite. See his 'Moral Principles and Inductive Policies' (Annual Philosophical Lecture to the British Academy, 1950) and 'An Empiricist's View of the Nature of Religious Belief' (Eddington Lecture, Cambridge, 1955).

G

matter of morality, and rules, unless they are self-evident or purely authoritarian (neither of which bases we have found plausible), find their justification in their context. Thus when *reasons* for actions have to be given, appeal to a rule, when pressed, will be likely to turn into an appeal to the purposes and interests the rule is held to serve. Yet there can sometimes be a propulsion to or revulsion from a course of conduct which seems like a 'Yes' or 'No' of one's basic attitude or orientation, where one is not prepared to discuss and weigh reasons — in an impulse to generosity, for instance, or a reaction to cruelty. When this point is reached, I do not think that Rule Utilitarianism with its appeal to reasons serves us. The more purely personal the morality, the more immediate is likely to be an expression of what is held to be a good kind of human relationship in itself, rather than a consideration of interests or wider social concern. These come in when we must think about reasons for our actions, and make moral judgments.

It seems, then, that neither an ethics of rules, nor of ends, nor calculation of consequences, can be simply applied to give sufficient answers to the question, 'What ought I to do?' There is no way of evading the need for moral *judgment*, fallible but like other skills capable of improvement through exercise, and particularly through exercise in difficult situations. Except in cases such as I have mentioned, where a final propulsion or repulsion seems to leave nothing to be said, judgment works through clear thinking about purposes, consequences, interests, needs, for others as for oneself. It can be guided by the spirit or orientation with which a person approaches moral questions, and by his perception of the kind of conduct through which this may be specified. More generally, it has the guiding lights of fairness and disinterested sympathy, which (if what I have said about Universalizability is acceptable) are the moral qualities in which practical reason comes to life.

CHAPTER FIVE

MORAL RELATIVISM

I HAVE tried to say something in general about how I think moral judgment operates; I shall now turn to ask what relevance sociological studies of social situations may have to the practical and theoretical problems which it raises. The first quick reply of the ordinary man, meaning someone who has not tried technically to become a moralist or a sociologist, is likely to be that of course any way of improving our knowledge of different kinds of people and how they live in their various social groups ought to improve our understanding of moral problems and making of moral judgments. Surely as we get to know more about people's notions of right and wrong and how they get on in their various 'experiments in living', we shall be better able to free ourselves from local prejudice, and be in a better position to weigh up alternative possibilities and decide what we really think is right and wrong. His next impression may, however, be less encouraging. Sociologists will describe the *mores* of a society as part of a whole culture, in which they are said to make sense as a whole, so that it looks as if they cannot be adopted in a piecemeal way by people of another culture without losing their point. Or, still more disturbingly, sociologists may tell him that if you occupy a certain position in a network of social relationships within a certain kind of society, you will have a certain moral outlook. And then what happens to your broadminded freedom of choice?

There is no doubt that a sociological approach can pull us towards determinism and moral relativism. Some Idealist philosophers have held a doctrine of 'internal relations', according to which the world is thought of as a system in which everything is so related to everything else, that nothing can be understood except with reference to its total context, every part of which contributes to making it what it is, so that it cannot be transposed to another context without becoming something different. It might be said that sociology is the contemporary refuge of the doctrine of internal relations.[1] It deals in networks of reciprocal relationships, in which the *mores* of a society are seen as integrated with other aspects of the society — its kinship system, its ways of getting a living, its ecology. Thus people's ethical beliefs and practice are seen in the context of their culture and ways of life and the structural forms in which these are organized, and this contextual way of looking at them is commonly taken to imply 'moral relativism'. A practice may be right in one social context and wrong in another; it would be meaningless to ask whether it is right or wrong in an abstract 'absolute' sense. As Sumner succinctly put it 'The *mores* can make anything right'.

I believe that, when people use the expression 'moral relativism', there is a tangle of different things which they may mean. To assent to some of these need not be to assent to others, and some distinctions must therefore be made. The word 'relativism' in itself suggests that something is regarded as related to something else, whereas 'absolute' literally and originally means that something stands in its own right, '*absolutum*', 'absolved' and free from dependence on anything outside itself. This presumably is why the nineteenth-century Idealists called their 'Ultimate Reality', seen as the *total* system of internal relations, 'The Absolute'. If something, x, is taken to be related to something else, y (here called the relatum), this can mean that the relation is one of functional dependence. That is, the

---

[1] This of course gets qualified in practice (see below, p. 139), and some things may make a lot of difference, some very little.

relatum calls the tune. x will vary systematically in accordance with variations in y. The value of x can be determined, for instance, if we know that $x = 2y$, and are given a value for y, so that x is interpreted as a function of y. The relation might, however, be looked on as one of reciprocal dependence: variations in x would be accompanied systematically by variations in y, and variations in y by variations in x, without saying which is the 'dependent' variable. This suggests two ways in which the relation of moral ideas and practices to other factors in their cultural context might be regarded. Let us call them respectively 'hard' and 'soft' relativism.

Relativism in the 'hard' form would be the view that moral principles are causally dependent on something else, e.g. inter-familial relationships, or early training within a particular culture, or on the form taken by the economic or power structure of a society at any time. In a 'soft' form it would be the view that, although there are distinctive moral factors, these are interrelated within a culture with other factors, such as familial, economic or power factors, so that they vary according to these. The difference between the 'hard' and 'soft' forms of relativism would be that for the former, morality is a resultant of other things; for the latter, there are genuine moral elements in a culture, but the form these take will be affected by other elements and vice versa, while the whole complex will make up a particular culture with its social structure. I do not mind saying that the 'soft' form of relativism seems to me the more plausible. It is also in effect the kind which fits best with the sociological outlook. For this, in most of the contemporary work at any rate, is seldom concerned to show all other factors in a culture as dependent on one dominant factor, such as the form of economic production, so much as to show how a number of factors mutually condition each other. This is how, for instance, Max Weber's well-known view of a nexus between the Protestant Ethic and early capitalist economic life can be taken.[1] This has often been discussed, and criticized in detail. But the criticisms have often proceeded on the assumption that Weber is making the form of the ethical life dependent on the economic, or vice versa, rather than taking what is to my mind the more fruitful view of mutual conditioning of one by the other. This mutual conditioning means also mutual reinforcement; when the conduct prescribed by two strong interests, such as the religious and the economic, points in the same direction so that the motives for the one reinforce instead of conflicting with the motives for the other, then a 'way of life' may get established with very strong power of survival — and who will say the Puritan way of life was not this? Sociologists are interested in seeing a nexus of this kind; indeed it is a multi-relational nexus of different factors that comprises what they understand by a culture. To see such a connection is not to say that religion, morality, economic life, and the rest may not have their own characteristic interests and purposes. It is to assert that the form these take is partly at any rate affected by the form the others are taking in the total way of life. Thus the 'softer' form of relativism is not committed to denying that there may be special ethical interests and motives; it is only committed to saying that the form of their expression and the behaviour to which they give rise is conditioned by other factors in their social context. This might be held nowadays to be almost a truism; but if we accept it, we have still not done with the different meanings of 'relativism'.

Another distinction to note is that between descriptive and normative relativism.[2] By 'descriptive relativism' is meant the empirical fact that people's moral principles and convictions are found to vary in different periods and cul-

[1] *The Protestant Ethic and the Spirit of Capitalism* (English translation by T. Parsons. London, 1930).

[2] On the distinction so drawn, cf. John Ladd, *The Structure of a Moral Code*, p. 322.

tures. By 'normative relativism' is meant that the actual rightness or wrongness of actions is relative. These two kinds of relativism do not imply each other. For it is possible that, though empirically there is a variety of different principles and convictions, nevertheless one set is actually right and the rest mistaken. Or it is possible that none of these is actually right, but nevertheless there is an ideal set of absolutely right principles which no one as yet possesses. This disparity between descriptive and normative relativism follows if we accept the logical distinction between what ought to be and what is. That there are some actions which ought to be done need not be defeated by the discovery that people have different views as to what these are. So one can be a descriptive relativist and a normative absolutist. Nevertheless, there are difficulties in this combination. For either one has to say that one set of moral principles is privileged (one's own?) or one has to say that we do not know which, if any, of the extant principles are actually right, though we believe there could be a code of such principles. I do not think that a person ought to say that he knew what these principles were, but that no one, including himself, held them, or knew he ought to do so, since it follows analytically from the meaning of 'knowing that a principle is right' that one acknowledges one ought to hold it. This does not of course mean that one would necessarily act on it. However, it is theoretically possible to be a descriptive relativist in giving accounts of *mores* and a normative absolutist in one's own moral philosophy. A position commonly met lies between the two; the principles I hold are normatively right for me, but others may be right for other people, especially those of other cultures, so I should not press my moral views on them. This raises the question of whether the diversity of *mores* is unlimited, or whether there are some principles which all men everywhere subscribe to, though perhaps under different forms; this would be a notion of 'Natural Law'. It also raises the question of whether, even if there is an unlimited variety of *mores*, there may nevertheless be reasons internal to morality itself for preferring some to others, apart from the consideration that one set of *mores* may be 'a poor thing but mine own'.

Whether or not the case for infinite variety is borne out by anthropological evidence is an empirical question; it could never be completely answered unless the evidence were complete. Similarly, the contrary, which we might call a natural law view based on a *consensus gentium*, could not be substantiated until we had a complete account of the moral principles of all the *gentes*, together with the knowledge that they were exhaustive — an induction by complete enumeration — and, as many societies have by now disappeared, this is in the nature of the case impossible. So all that the advocates of a 'natural law' or 'natural morality' view can maintain is that there is evidence either for a substantial agreement on basic moral principles, or for such agreement amongst people who reflect rationally on their principles. Whether the former alternative can be sustained is an empirical question for the social anthropologists. An amateur reader of their work may however note that the tendency in recent anthropological writing about ethics seems to be much less extremely relativistic than that of a generation ago. This may be partly because, writing in an age where the prevalent assumptions about ethics are relativistic in any case, anthropologists to-day need not be concerned, as one suspects some of their forebears were, to shake Victorian absolutes. It may also be because a more detailed understanding of the working of the *mores* shows that there are some needs and purposes which a moral system has to fulfil, and that therefore the rationale of even at first sight very divergent practices may not be so very different in context. What Duncker[1] calls the 'situational meaning' of a phrase such as 'killing an aged

[1] Cf. K. Duncker, 'Ethical Relativity?', *Mind* (1939), N.S. vol. XLVIII, pp. 39–57.

parent' may differ when account is taken of the motives, reasons and symbolic beliefs of the group in question. Limitations on 'the Diversity of Morals'[1] may thus be due to considerations of what, with the support of Professor H. L. A. Hart,[2] I shall dare to call 'natural necessities'. Whatever else morals may be concerned with, they are concerned with ways in which people live together in some form of ordered society. There may be some requirements for this which depend on constant facts about human society — Hart lists the desire for survival, restrictions on violence, some notion of property and some co-operation in a coercive order. Clyde Kluckhohn[3] goes further and suggests that every culture will need to have a conception of murder as distinct from justifiable homicide; some notion of incest and other regulations of sexual behaviour; prohibition of untruth under defined circumstances (the operative word here is 'defined'); reciprocity of obligations, especially obligations of parents to children and vice versa. This has been put so well by Abraham and May Edel that I shall quote what they say at length: 'The patterns of human social interaction, however deep their biological and psychological roots, are not simply direct instinctual expression, or the playing out of a built-in psychological drama. They are, as Kluckhohn puts it, "somewhat distinct answers to essentially the same questions posed by human biology and by the generalities of the human situation". They are complex answers, ways which have been built up over time, "experiments in living", to use Macbeath's telling phrase, that different cultures have

[1] The phrase is M. Ginsberg's ; see his *Essays in Sociology and Social Philosophy* (London, 1956), vol. I.

[2] See *The Concept of Law* (Oxford, 1961), p. 195.

[3] 'Ethical Relativity: Sic et Non' in the Symposium. 'Ethical Relativity in the Light of Recent Developments in Social Science' (American Philosophical Association, Eastern Division, 1955) (*Journal of Philosophy*, LII, pp. 663–677).

worked out, in the course of which new and varying needs have themselves been generated. There is room for wide variety in the kinds of lives men build for themselves, but certain minimal standards must be met if these "experiments" are to be successful at all. Each culture must provide patterns of motor habits, social relations, knowledge and beliefs, such that it will be possible for men to survive. Everywhere there must be techniques for making a living, patterns of mating, of mutual help, ways of defining who is a friend and who a foe, and of dealing with each, ways of coping with sickness and old age and death — and means for learning all of these ways. And there are not only common requirements imposed by common problems, but common psychological processes and mechanisms through which they operate and on which they react. Birth and death, love and sorrow and fear are the lot of all men; all are capable of desires and dreams, and use symbolic thinking, identification, reaction-formation. This common human nature sets limits to the forms that any experiments in living can take, to the possible techniques of motivation, the scope of sympathy, the effectiveness of sanctions.

'Common needs, common social tasks, common psychological processes, are bound to provide some common framework for the wide variety of human behaviours that different cultures have developed. And part of this framework includes the need for a certain measure of co-operation and conformity in the behaviour of the members of any society. Those who live and work together must go along the paths charted by the customs and expectations of the group not just through external coercive pressures but through motivations which are to some degree built into their habits and attitudes.'[1]

[1] May Edel and Abraham Edel, *Anthropology and Ethics*, pp. 30–31 (American Lecture Series, No. 353). Quoted by courtesy of Charles C. Thomas, Publisher, Springfield, Illinois, and of Professor A. Edel. For 'functional requisites' for a society, see M. I. Levi,

To say that any moral system will be concerned to meet these needs somehow or other and be concerned with viable ways in which people can live together may surely be granted. It does not foreclose any possibilities of moral concerns beyond this; as Aristotle remarked long ago, people come together for the sake of life, and then go on to develop 'the good life'. Nor does it rule out the possibility that any given moral system may include a number of practices which can hardly be justified in terms of either 'life' or 'good life'. They may be there for a variety of extraneous reasons: mistaken beliefs about matter of fact, and 'superstitions' in the original sense of survivals remaining from inertia. It was no doubt a healthy reaction on the part of functional anthropologists against a morally superior attitude to 'the beastly devices of the heathen' to try to see every practice as contributing to some useful purpose, or to the general purpose of keeping going the society's way of life. This can of course be tautological, if the 'way of life' is defined as the sum total of the practices. But it need not be. 'Survival' need not mean that everything continues as it is — it may also mean adaptation to change. And some societies do not survive. So the notion of survival must be distinguished from the mere perpetuation of the whole given assemblage of institutions and customs, and it must be possible at least to entertain the possibility that some of them serve no useful purpose, or that they could be replaced by others.[1]

Hence when Professor Macbeath reiterates that practices

The Structure of Society (Princeton, 1953), Chapter IV; and on a more abstract level, T. Parsons, R. F. Bales and E. A. Shils, _Working Papers in the Theory of Action_ (Chicago, Free Press, 1953), pp. 180–190, on the requisites of adaptation, goal gratification and integration.

[1] On this, see R. K. Merton, 'Manifest and Latent Functions' in _Social Theory and Social Structure_ (2nd edition, 1957), pp. 19–84.

are to be seen as right because they are seen as contributing
to a way of life that commends itself as good to the people
of the society concerned, this is surely an overstatement
of what is, I believe, basically a sound point of view.[1]
Some practices may continue just from inertia, i.e., they
have always been done before, and we have not thought of
anything else to do. If 'the *mores* can make anything
right', it may still be the case, as Professor Redfield, quoting
Robert E. Park, remarks, that the *mores* have a harder time
making some things right than others.[2]

We are still talking in terms of 'descriptive relativism'.
Limitations to an infinite diversity of *mores* set by biological
and social necessities still allow for wide variation, and we
are still far from saying whether there are any fundamental
and universal moral rules. As an appeal to a *consensus
gentium* this is an empirical question, which fits Professor
Popper's view of a scientific hypothesis, in being capable
of falsification but not verification.[3] But even if no such
consensus gentium can be established, this need not commit
us to being 'normative relativists'. We could still believe
that a certain rule was 'right', not only 'right for us', and
not be shaken by finding that the Kavirondo would not
agree. This follows from the logical distinction between

[1] See his *Experiments in Living, passim.* One of the clearest
statements of this kind of view, not written from anthropological
interest, is H. W. B. Joseph's *Some Problems in Ethics* (Oxford,
1931).

[2] *The Little Community* (Uppsala and Chicago, 1955), p. 48. The
context is where Redfield writes 'You recognize that if you were a
younger son who had spent years in learning from your father the
sacred lore that would qualify you to assume his respected office, then,
even though the social structure told you that as the younger brother
the chieftainship was not for you, when you found yourself put aside
for, of all people, your older brother, a man who had gone off and
abandoned his plain duty, you would feel wronged. Anybody would,
one declares, social structure or no social structure.'

[3] See his *The Logic of Scientific Enquiry* (London, 1959) *passim.*

statements of what is the case and statements of what ought
to be done. (How many of us in fact arrive at moral convictions inductively by looking for agreements in different
cultures? And would we be shaken in a conviction that,
e.g., gratuitous cruelty was wrong by reading of a tribe
that thought differently?)

If this is so, one's reasons for being or not being a normative relativist will turn on *philosophical* views about ethics,
and not on empirical discoveries about the diversity of
morals. By a philosophical view, I understand a view of
the nature of ethical judgment including questions such as
what kind of assertion an ethical assertion is. If I say '*x* is
right' am I saying something true or false in a sense which
in any way parallels the factual truth or falsity of a statement
such as '*x* is square'? Obviously, if we can say this, the
relativist case falls. On the other hand if I say '*x* is right'
means '*x* seems right to me', and that '*x* is square' means
'*x* looks square to me', the parallel can be seen not to hold.
For there are intersubjective methods of measurement by
which even if an area *looks* oblong to some observers, it
can be shown to answer to a description of square which
they would all accept. What is the independent measure
of what is to count as right? This might be said to be
rational intuition — self evidence. There must then presumably be an appeal to further intuition to judge which is
the more stringent principle in cases of conflict. One
trouble (there may be many more) about an appeal to self-
evident intuition is that it is vulnerable to the challenge of
anyone who says that these principles are not self-evident
to *him*. I remember the shocked exasperation with which
the late H. A. Prichard used to meet this kind of objection.
They must surely in the end, he would say, be evident to
any right-minded and mature person. Though the discovery of different moral notions among different peoples
need not *disprove* ethical intuitionism it does make it im-
plausible, and seems to call for a highly restrictive view of

who are to count as right-minded and morally mature people.[1]

Another possibility is that ethical assertions are assertions of approval or disapproval. This is the kind of view associated with the name of Westermarck among others, who significantly adds that approbation or disapprobation, if it is moral, is 'disinterested'. I can feel resentment or approval of an act apart from any reference it may have to me personally or to my own interests. Westermarck thus combines a view of the diversity of morals (it will be remembered that he calls one of his books *Ethical Relativity*) with a view of moral judgment, which sees it as 'subjective' in that it is an expression of feeling, and feelings belong to subjects, yet as having one of the characteristics of objective judgment, in that it must be impartial.

We can note in passing that there are ambiguities in the term 'subjective' used in talking about morals. It may mean:

(1) That moral judgment only gives information about a subject's state of mind (e.g. that he disapproves of something).

(2) That it gives no information, but expresses or evinces feelings; this may be combined with a prescriptive command (as in Stevenson's model where 'this is good' = 'I approve of this; do so as well').

(3) That it is only 'a matter of opinion' (i.e. no intersubjective criteria are possible).

(4) That you ought to do what you think is right: the notion of 'subjective duty'. This need not exclude

[1] The anthropologist R. R. Marett in speaking of Cook Wilson, a member of the same school as Prichard, says that Cook Wilson thought 'all this evolutionary stuff about ethics seemed rather pointless to him, as holding that ethical principles were demonstrably "there", though mankind might have indulged in all manner of false starts before debouching on to the highway of reason'. *A Jerseyman at Oxford* (Oxford, 1941), p. 118.

the possibility of there also being an objectively right act, though you may not know what it is.

'Objective' is similarly ambiguous. It may mean that moral judgments describe facts 'out there'; or it may mean that there are criteria in moral argument. 'Ideal Observer' views are thus subjective in so far as they evince a state of mind and objective in so far as they appeal to a particular (disinterested) state of mind as a criterion. Thus just to dub a moral view 'subjective' *tout court* can be highly misleading. So it is just to dub a view 'objective'. We have looked at the case for *procedural objectivity* — 'treat like cases alike, and different cases differently', i.e. act without special pleading, fear or favour — as a 'constitutive rule' for moral judgments in so far as we seek to make them rationally. I believe that a stronger case can be argued for what may be called 'natural procedural justice' than for natural law as a universal substantive code.[1] In this procedural sense, *justice* (that is, distributive rather than corrective justice) becomes a special sort of virtue, representing practical reason in its moral application. That there is something special about justice has haunted people from the Greeks onward. For Plato in the *Republic* δικαιοσύνη comes near to being a notion of what is right in general (we need not of course interpret it in his particular sense of willingness to accept an objectively calculated distribution of functions). But natural justice as procedural is fairness in the application of whatever rules we may have. It can be compatible with the most plausible form of relativism: the notion that in the context of a given way of life certain practices and rules are genuinely right for those whose way of life it is, whereas others would be right for others. This contextual, 'internal relations' view of moral rules and

---

[1] I have argued this more fully in *Justice and the Law* (Essex Hall Memorial Lecture, 1963). Cf. also H. L. A. Hart, *The Concept of Law*, p. 202, and above, pp. 79–80 *n*.

practices can make them both relative to context and, objective for that context. Its upshot would be that people, whether they be colonial administrators, missionaries or social workers, ought not to interfere with the *mores* of another people.

This raises the questions of judgments on 'ways of life'. Are they all equally commendable, or (what is not quite the same thing) all right for those who live them? Are they any good reasons for criticizing a way of life?

The best-known answer, saying 'No' to this, is probably Ruth Benedict's *Patterns of Culture*. Ruth Benedict describes three different cultures with great sympathy and perceptiveness. She sees them as 'equally valid patterns of life which mankind has created for itself from the raw materials of existence'.[1] Each has selected from among human 'potentialities'. Some 'potentialities' indeed she recognizes can only be realized at great cost, but 'if any society wishes to pay that cost for its chosen and congenial traits, certain values will develop within this pattern, however "bad" it may be'.[2] The test case is the account of the Dobu, a Polynesian people off south-east New Guinea studied by Dr. Rheo Fortune,[3] who have one of the 'patterns of culture' Ruth Benedict describes. The social *mores* of the Dobu put a premium on treachery, mutual ill-will and suspicion. Fear of sorcery and witchcraft permeates all their relationships; it does not seem, as with Professor Evans-Pritchard's Azande, to be directed only against those who on reasonably defensible grounds can be suspected of anti-social behaviour. Indeed, the description of Dobu society reads like a description of a paranoiac society in which anyone may be under suspicion. If you plant a tree, you put a curse laying a horrible disease on anyone who steals the fruit; but a thief will put a still more horrible counter-

---

[1] *Patterns of Culture* (English edition, London, 1935), p. 201.
[2] *Op. cit.* p. 179.
[3] *Sorcerers of Dobu* (London and New York, 1932).

curse on you. A thief, you may say, is up to no good anyhow; but even in intimate relations of marriage, each
spouse goes in continual fear of sorcery or witchcraft from
the other. It is indeed a society permeated by envy, hatred,
malice and all uncharitableness. Nevertheless, Ruth Benedict tries to put it beyond criticism as one of the ways of
managing life.[1] These paranoiac practices are said to have
the advantage that those prone to them, who would be
misfits in another culture, are at home among the Dobu.
'In Dobu those whose first impulse is to select a victim and
project their misery upon him in procedures of punishment
are equally fortunate', i.e. as fortunate as the Kwakiutl
Indians of the American North-West coast 'who can
assuage despair by the act of bringing shame on others'.[2]
It can of course be argued that the sorcery and witchcraft
practices of the Dobu are one of the ways in which people
keep themselves and their society ticking; but surely it
must at least be a very time-consuming way. Moreover,
we are told that their numbers are going down drastically.
Is this an effect of their fear-ridden way of life, or a cause
of it? Or is it, more probably, one of the 'vicious circle'
phenomena which sociologists are good at uncovering,
where one tendency reinforces another, so that the decrease
in numbers increases mutual fears, and vice versa?

Is it, then, possible to say that on the score of happiness
and of satisfactory human relationships some 'experiments
in living' are more successful than others? And is it possible
for some features of a 'way of life' to be criticized and
changed without bringing the whole thing down?

I suspect that the influence of Durkheim has led people
to look on a society's way of life as more tightly integrated,

[1] Dr. Fortune's account of the Dobu is the objective analysis of
an anthropologist, but without this parade of moral detachment and
even justification. It is evident that he both loved his unpleasant
Dobu and pitied their unhappiness.

[2] *Patterns of Culture*, p. 184.

H

and its morality as calling for closer conformity than need be the case. Durkheim indeed brought out the need for shared moral convictions and moral discipline if a society is to be stable. But there are ways of carrying a certain amount of instability and of resolving conflicts besides that of reasserting belief in a single existing set of *mores*. There may be different *mores* in sub-groups of the society; and the capacity to adapt to change may be a condition of stability which can depend on people being able to question some features of the *mores*. We have seen too that people may not always be prepared just to conform to what is traditional. They may ask 'Why should we?', and the hunt for reasons will be on. The reasons may not always seem very convincing. This may be because of strains in the society itself. One need not be a Thrasymachus or a Marxist to believe that the morality of a society is likely to be largely one that suits its dominant classes, if only because they have the main control over its educational institutions. So there may be protests on the part of submerged elements, perhaps appealing to egalitarian sentiments in the morality itself. There may also be the occasional radical with his odd point of view, epitomized by Flanders' and Swann's Reluctant Cannibal: 'Eating people is Wrong'. These are internal critical voices; there may also be external pressures from changing circumstances and wider cultural contacts — the problem of tribal moralities in societies which can no longer remain isolated. So among the questions that can be asked about a way of life is whether its maintenance depends on some elements being submerged, and whether it has resources for meeting the aspirations of these when they see a chance of change; also, whether it can adapt itself to other kinds of change by means other than defence mechanisms such as sorcery, which can at best maintain the *status quo*, and not help the society on to a new stage.

Thus even if moral beliefs and practices need to be seen

in their context, this does not necessarily mean that the *mores* must be just so for the society to survive, in any but the tautological sense in which the society is defined as that particular assemblage of *mores* — not, surely, a very helpful definition. In fact since, in the modern world at any rate, change is forced on people willy-nilly, it is truer to say with Burke that 'a state without the means of some change is without the means of its conservation'. Moreover, change may be met in a way which makes for the development of morality itself. This needs explaining, for we might say that all systems of morality are moral by definition, none more and none less, and call nothing human alien to us. If, however, morality is not only a matter of 'regulative' rules but also 'constitutive' principles according to which moral judgments are made, and if the making of judgments is not just an automatic reckoning, but a skill, then these principles can be used more and less intelligently, and provide clues as to how moral judgments can be made better. (There may be force in the dictum of the ancient Protagoras, that though no moral judgment may be more *true* than another, one may be *better* than another.) We noted one such constitutive principle in the 'Universalizability' test of rational consistency, 'Treat like cases alike and different cases differently', developed in moral thinking into the 'Golden Rule', interpreted as 'Treat other people according to the principles on which you would wish to be treated yourself'. This is likely to react in criticism on systems of *mores* where there are exploited groups, since few of us are prepared to be Hare's 'fanatics', prepared to be exploited were we members of such a group.[1] 'Universalizability', though in itself it only says rules should be applied consistently, is thus capable of leading on by an internal logic, to a *universalizing* of obligations because discriminatory treatment has to be justified. Another guiding light can be the Hobbesian principle, by which morality is

[1] *Freedom and Reason*, Chapter IX.

seen as having the function of enabling people to live together with sufficient mutual trust to be able to form reasonable expectations that they will behave peaceably. This could develop so as to encourage qualities which enlarge possibilities of trust, making possible co-operative enterprises. Such trust could improve people's resourcefulness not only in seizing the main chance, but in dealing together with the problems set by changing circumstances.

All this indicates a direction of development in morality, rather than a single universal moral code. It is a direction for which we can find independent support in Piaget's studies of the moral development of children.[1] Piaget discerns three different attitudes to rules, corresponding to stages in a child's development. The first is the repetitive 'ritualistic' following of a rule, as when a small child in a game throws a marble again and again. The second is where the rule is seen as externally imposed and changeless, and to follow it is a matter of sheer obedience or disobedience. The third is where rules are seen as reciprocal agreements enabling people to do things together, whether playing a game or planning a holiday. Piaget agrees with Durkheim that rules and moral habits are transmitted through social pressure and training, and are not a matter of biological instinct, so that human life is inescapably social. But Piaget says that Durkheim's view of the functioning of moral rules in society follows the first two of these stages, with little notice of the third. Also Durkheim talks of the characteristics of social restraint in terms of the kinds of pressure adults bring to bear on small children and the psychological aftermath of these. He does not have much to say about the possibility of morality developing through rational co-operation, except where incidentally he notes that the 'Division of Labour', by breaking up 'mechanical

[1] Cf. J. Piaget, *The Moral Judgment of the Child* (English translation, London, 1932).

solidarity' and producing a differentiated society, can encourage liberation of individual minds. Piaget also notes that Durkheim talks only about adult society or adults disciplining children; he does not consider the society of children with other children, for instance in their games, out of which the third attitude can be seen beginning to grow as they become more sophisticated in their play. Piaget also notes the strong sense of justice in children, and the stages by which it develops as (i) a subordination to adult authority: even at this stage a small child will feel a sense of injustice if the adults do not stick to their own rules; (ii) sheer egalitarianism — 'it isn't fair that he should have more than me'; (iii) egalitarianism tempered by equity where (about the age of 11–12) a child sees that smaller or weaker ones should have special consideration; in other words, the rules of purely egalitarian justice can be qualified where there are *reasons* for differential treatment. Piaget believes that there is a rational development in all this, whereby 'Reciprocity imposes itself on practical reason as logical principles impose themselves morally on theoretical reason'.[1] Of course the children he was observing were Genevan children, brought up in the moral culture of Western Europe. It would be very interesting if his collaborators could show whether there is evidence for similar stages and attitudes among children of other cultures. In any case, he has convincingly shown a rationale in these stages of development towards a freer, more autonomous use of rules in practical reason.

So if we are asked summarily whether morality is 'absolute' or 'relative', it will not be possible to answer without making a good many distinctions. Particular moral rules may indeed make sense in the context of some kinds of social situation and not in others. But this does not imply an infinite diversity of morals, leaving us with only emotional preference or tradition to decide between them. Morality

[1] *Op. cit.* p. 316.

can be a matter of judgment. There may be better and worse judgments within the same social contexts; every society can have its men of practical wisdom. There may be ways of life which allow for the development of moral judgment better than others do. Although judgment is guided by rules, it does not simply apply them automatically. Moral judgment remains problematic; it is indeed possible that skill in making moral judgments can grow through facing the fact that they are problematic. To face them responsibly is to approach them as *moral* problems, without special pleading, fear or favour. It is also to face them as moral *problems* where the answer is not always given by just looking up the local book of rules.

CHAPTER SIX

SOCIOLOGICAL EXPLANATION
AND
INDIVIDUAL RESPONSIBILITY

To speak of a person facing moral problems as both moral and problematic is to assume that he has some capacity for using his judgment and making decisions. This assumption can produce a second worry for someone who looks at sociology and indeed psychology with an initial presumption that they ought to be able to help him in moral decisions. The first worry, 'Relativism', we have seen need only be destructive of moral judgment if we are unable to distinguish between conformity to *mores* and critical appraisals. But is this distinction realistic, at any rate in a sense in which it leaves room for individual decisions? Sociologists, and in other ways psychologists, may be able to show an individual as being a certain kind of person in a certain kind of situation; they may be able to explain why certain kinds of decisions are made by certain kinds of people and predict what they will be. If some people do not seem to be true to type, this may be explained too by showing how they form a sub-type. Then does sociological explanation commit us to determinism and to denying personal responsibility?

A short way with this is a form of the 'autonomy of ethics'; different ways of talking are distinguished, and we are told not to mix them up. There is a neuro-physiological account of behaviour, in terms of electrical discharges and motor reaction. There is a sociological account of behaviour in terms of roles correlated with positions in a social structure; and there is an account of human actions in terms of purposes, intentions, responsibility. All is well, provided we know which 'language game' we are playing, and do not confuse one with another.[1] But we are not only concerned to play language games; we are concerned with how things are, and in the nature of things there are cross-references. Can conscious purposive action make a difference to events in the empirical world, so that if I decide to walk across the room, the spatio-temporal disposition of certain neuro-physiological patterns of events will be different from what they would have been otherwise? On the other hand, cannot the biochemical action of drugs impair my powers of decision? In any case, decisions have to be taken in situations which, whatever else they may be, are states of affairs in the empirical world, where events can provide reasons (even if not final ones) for decisions. So a moralist cannot live in a world of free action in splendid isolation from empirical considerations. Nor, as we saw, can sociologists say they are only concerned to talk about social phenomena in a way that insulates them from moral decisions. The separation of 'two languages', while it can be methodologically useful, cannot therefore be finally serious. Both moralists and sociologists are put on the spot over the need to understand facts of the empirical world and over the question of personal responsibility. For moralists, this complicates the practical problem of deciding what ought to be done (it would be simpler if it were only a matter of following pure *a priori* principles); and also produces the logical problem of the bearing of what is on what ought to be. For sociologists, it may impose something of a dilemma of conscience. They may believe that to relax a deterministic view of sociological explanation of human action would be to betray their claim to scientific status. Yet in thinking about the applications of their finds in social

[1] A. I. Melden's view in *Free Action* (London, 1961) is a form of this view; and so in effect is Kant's distinction between the self as phenomenally determined and as noumenally free.

policies, these same sociologists will stress their responsibility as men and citizens. There seems to be a split here between the role of a sociologist *qua* scientist and *qua* citizen. If this were simply a distinction of roles, it might be defended (though we saw reasons in Chapter II for asking whether it can finally be sustained). But it looks more like a situation in which a sociologist combines free will for himself, in the sense of believing that he can make responsible decisions, with determinism for other people whose actions he believes he can explain and even predict.

Can sociological explanation be both serious and informative, and yet not leave those who give it in this dilemma? What sort of explanation is it? Is it compatible with believing that there is scope for individuals to use their initiative to make decisions?

We start from 'the Self as Agent'.[1] We are aware of manipulating things before we start classifying them. The child explores the world around him before he learns language. He acts and is acted on, wants something, and is often frustrated in trying to get it. Along with the power of language, but perhaps even before it, he acquires anticipations of what may happen. He also becomes conscious of his own actions and can enjoy repeating them, for instance triumphantly throwing his toy out of the pram. From such beginnings we presumably go on to awareness of ourselves acting purposively in our environment, an awareness we presuppose in everyday conduct as well as in ordinary language. This does not seem to be awareness of a specific introspectable voluntary act as a cause setting in motion, e.g., the raising of my arm.[2] Rather, I am aware of moving my arm intentionally. An *intentional action* has been defined by Miss Anscombe [3] as (*a*) a sub-class of the actions of

---

[1] The title of a book by John Macmurray, the first volume of his Gifford Lectures, *The Form of the Personal* (London, 1961).

[2] Cf. Gilbert Ryle, *The Concept of Mind* (numerous editions), *passim*.

[3] *Intention* (Blackwell, Oxford, 1957).

which we are aware otherwise than by observation (the whole class would include, e.g., reflexes): I do not see my arm move and say 'hullo, I must have intended to move it'. (*b*) It is an action for which a 'why' which is not a causal 'why' is appropriate. An answer to 'why' in the case of an intentional action refers to an objective. So if I say 'I am going for a walk' and you ask me 'why?', to say 'To get exercise' would sound a sensible explanation. But if I say 'I am going to be sick', to ask for an objective by way of explanation would not sound sensible. The teleological answer to 'why?' assumes the capacity to entertain an objective and to act in order to get it. Now we are told that scientists should eschew teleological explanations; yet the pursuit of science itself is a purposive activity on the part of the scientist, notably when he sets up an experiment or makes an observation in order to test something. Can there be scientific *explanation*, in a world in which there are also scientific *experiments*? Surely, or there would be no future in science. And where the subject matter to be 'explained' is human social action, since it is not plausible to think that the sociologist seeking to explain this is the only person capable of purposive action, there must be some way of allowing both for the possibility of purposive action and of finding scope for sociological explanation.

Our difficulties may partly be due to an implicit assumption that the model for explanation ought to be the old type of physical causal determinism, to which Laplace gave classical expression, when he claimed that from a knowledge of the physico-chemical laws of the particles making up the universe, and from their position at a given time, the future state of the universe could in principle be predicted. This must be looked on as a programmatic pronouncement, not a scientific hypothesis, since it cannot be verified or falsified (how could one get the position of *all* the particles, knowing it was a complete account?). A programmatic pronouncement serves as a policy directive, not as a statement of fact. Here the policy could be one of reduction: explain the behaviour of things in terms of the physics and chemistry of the fundamental particles. But nowadays this could not give us the old model of determinism, for the laws of the physics of particles are not now seen as the strict causal laws of classical mechanics. The latter are applicable to large-scale physical bodies in motion; the movements and positions of constituent particles are described statistically by probabilities. Indeed, these latter cannot be calculated by the same operation, since the operations needed to discover the velocity upset the position, and vice versa. This is the Principle of Indeterminacy (or Uncertainty). It does not say that individual particles have 'free will'; indeed we do not know what analogy there may be, if any, between their behaviour and human actions. But it limits powers to describe the behaviour of individual particles, and so makes a break with the rigid deterministic philosophy of nature. It also means the presence and action of the observer must be taken into account.

Another difference between the outlook of the old mechanistic determinism and more modern views is the importance of the notion of ordered systems. Organization is certainly a feature of biological organisms; it may also be a feature of the systems in fundamental particles. An ordered system is structured in a way which canalizes its energy input as 'information', so that its output is of a specific patterned kind, including 'feed-backs', or corrections of imbalance. The contemporary interest in systems with feed-backs may be producing new sets of analogies between the different kinds of system found in nature: indeed, the notion of a flow-back of information was familiar in the social sciences before the rise of 'Information Theory' in the technical sense. It is questionable, however, whether social 'systems' are as unified as are natural systems or humanly made artefacts. Be this as it may, the two notions, statistical laws and ordered system,

open up ways of thinking about social order and its regularities and deviations which are potentially more interesting
than analogies drawn from the old-fashioned classical
mechanics.

There are, then, forms of scientific explanation that use
more complex notions than simple efficient causality. They
may even help one day over the age-old 'body-mind' problem. The notion of the mind as producing acts of will
triggering off bodily movements may well be a relic of the
older views of efficient causation; and indeed for other
reasons it is out of favour with most contemporary philosophers. This may give way to a view of the whole person
as embodied mind, or 'imminded body', acting as a system
which has become *conscious*, and, because conscious, capable
of awareness of goals and of self-steering to reach them.
Of course what goals and what means of reaching them are
possible will depend upon the physical make-up of the
organism. I could not run a mile in four minutes (or indeed
in any number of minutes), and no one can run one in four
seconds. But, within limits, a number of things may be
possible; athletes can train themselves to run a mile in four
minutes and under. Also, as they say, you sometimes
don't know what you can do till you try; and you sometimes
manage to try harder than you thought you could.

The moral of this is that we should get away from talking
about a 'free will' as though it were an organ inside a
person, like a 'free wheel' on a bicycle (though of course
with a different function), and of consciousness as belonging
to a 'Ghost' seated somewhere in the 'machine'.[1] Indeed,
the common expression 'seat of consciousness' is misleading. My St. John Ambulance first aid handbook describes
the brain as 'the seat of intellect, the emotions and the will'.
Of course consciousness depends on the functioning of the
higher nervous centres, but is it 'seated' there? As Dr.

[1] 'The Ghost in the Machine': a phrase Professor Ryle has put
into circulation.

Austin Farrer has remarked 'consciousness cannot sit down, not having the wherewithal'.[1] He goes on to speak of how a tennis player's intelligence can be expressed in the turn of his wrist; his attention is centred on the ball, and not on forming an 'act of volition' in his mind to trigger off an event in his brain to connect with his wrist. It is surely less misleading to think of the person as a whole as acting consciously, intelligently, voluntarily. As Locke put it, we should ask not whether the will is free but whether the man is free. So questions about purposive action can be reworded in terms of the capacities of the embodied person as a whole to envisage objectives and set himself to achieve them.

We shall allow, then, that there can be goal-seeking activities, and consciousness of goals (indeed the experience is so compelling that we can hardly deny it). The determinist difficulty is not so much over this kind of purposive action: it is rather over whether, with complete psychological and sociological understanding, it should be possible to deduce just what goals a person would entertain.

Then would a statement like 'I am going for a walk' not in fact be a statement of intention to follow a chosen course, but a prediction of the action to which my present state is going to lead me (as in 'I am going to be sick')? Professor D. M. MacKay has drawn attention to an operational difference between a statement of intention and a prediction, in that if you tell me 'You are about to go for a walk', my knowing what you predict (granted that I am not being hypnotized) enables me to do something else: 'all right then, I won't'.[2] A psychologist might take care of this by appealing to contrasuggestibility; he could know that his telling a person he is about to do something (Prediction₁)

---

[1] *The Freedom of the Will* (London, 1958), p. 24.
[2] See 'Body and Mind, Readings in Philosophy' edited by G. N. A. Vesey (London, 1964), pp. 392 ff. The origin of the argument is attributed to Professor Popper (p. 394).

would introduce a new variable which would induce him to do something else (Prediction $_2$). The psychologist might be able to predict what this would be, but he would have to keep it to himself and not tell the subject. So the scientist's genuine prediction would be Prediction $_2$. But if I told myself in making Prediction $_1$ that I was going to act in accordance with Prediction $_2$, I could then decide to do something else (Prediction $_3$), and so on in an infinite regress. As agent, I can always be one step ahead of any proffered prediction.

So far as human actions are concerned, there is also a logical problem in the correlation between prediction and what it is correct to believe. If I predict an eclipse correctly, I would also be correct in believing the prediction. But suppose a human action where one condition of the action occurring is that the agent believes it will happen. Then we get the paradoxical situation that he will not be in error if he disbelieves the prediction, since if he disbelieves it, it will fail. So we cannot say, as in the case of the eclipse, that the prediction is logically binding in the sense that the agent would be correct if he believed it, and incorrect if he did not.[1] Similarly, if a condition of the action occurring is that the agent does *not* believe it will occur, then he will be in error if he believes the prediction that it will occur. So to see that the agent has the power to change the validity of the prediction, it is not even necessary to *tell* him what it is. It is sufficient to see that the prediction is not logically binding on him in the sense that he would be correct in believing and incorrect in disbelieving it, or vice versa.

R. K. Merton has called attention to a possible outcome of predictions about the results of actions on a large scale by

[1] This point is made by D. M. MacKay in a paper 'Information and Prediction in the Human Sciences', in *Information and Prediction in Science*, ed. Dockx and Bernays (Academic Press, New York, 1965).

speaking of the 'self-fulfilling' or 'self-defeating prophecy'.[1] The fact that a prediction has been made may encourage people so to act that it is more likely to be true: if this happens in the case of predictions of election results, it is called the 'bandwagon' effect. When people are more likely to vote for a candidate when they expect him to lose, this is called the 'underdog effect'. H. A. Simon [2] has argued that it might be possible *in principle* to take account of reactions to a published prediction in such a way that the prediction would be confirmed by the event. But the words 'in principle' are important; and it is recognized that the publication of the prediction itself introduces a new variable into the situation, which can affect the outcome in more than one way. If a prediction can produce complacency or fear, it might discourage people from acting in the way required for it to be fulfilled — this can be called a 'boomerang' response.[3]

Perhaps, however, there need not be a tie-up of determinism with the possibility of prediction. I can predict with virtual certainty that you are not going to murder me in the next few minutes, but perhaps you *could* do so. There was a character in one of Dostoevsky's stories who committed suicide just so as to show that he could do it. Also some of the people we look on as the strongest characters are the most dependable in some of their actions; we know the sort of things they would think too silly or despicable to do. So the determinism-freewill contrast and the possibility or impossibility of prediction are not exactly parallel. For

[1] Cf. R. K. Merton, *Social Theory and Social Structure*, Chapter XI, pp. 421 ff. (I repeat 'on a large scale'. An individual, if he is prepared to be sophisticated, might defeat a prediction in the way MacKay says, in so far as it affected himself.)

[2] Cf. H. A. Simon, *Models of Man*, Chapter V, 'Bandwagon and Underdog Effects of Election Predictions' (New York, 1957).

[3] Cf. R. K. Merton and Patricia L. Kendall, 'The Boomerang Response', *Channels*, vol. XXI, no. 7 (National Publicity Council).

the question of free will is not a question of indeterminism, or of a subject being able to do anything whatsoever, but the question of whether he can at all direct his energies and control his feelings through conscious deliberation. One form of this would be what Professor Findlay calls 'cool wanting': an orientation by which a person can plan things he is not immediately and actively wanting *now*; one sense of 'will power' may be the ability to hold on to these long-term 'cool wants'.[1] Or the kind of thinking involved may be a recollection of what is considered appropriate and inappropriate (compare the meaning of 'I want' in 'I want to be sick', and 'I don't want to be sick *here* — in public'). 'Wanting' is not therefore just a simple brute fact, acting as irresistible cause. It can be emphasized or inhibited. Indeed, to say that we are bound to follow the strongest impulse may be a dogmatic belief, but is not a scientific hypothesis apart from some means of measuring the strength of impulses independently of seeing which one was followed, and making that the strongest by definition. There is the same difficulty over the notion of 'irresistible impulse' as a plea for 'diminished responsibility' in criminal law. How does one know that an impulse was irresistible and not only not resisted, for how can one verify the counter-factual 'He could not have resisted it if he had tried'? So, wisely, the Homicide Act of 1957 did not make use of this notion, but tried to specify kinds of mental and emotional condition short of 'insanity' as defined by the M'Naghten rules,[2] as likely to make for 'diminished responsibility'. Some penal

---

[1] See J. A. Findlay, *Values and Intentions* (London, 1961). William James' interpretation of 'will' as the capacity to hold an idea in consciousness in spite of distractions is a similar view; cf. his chapter on 'The Will' in *Principles of Psychology* (numerous editions).

[2] By which a man was held responsible unless the case could be made out that he could not have known that what he was doing was wrong. On this whole question, see the *Report of the Royal Commission on Capital Punishment* (H.M.S.O. 1953).

reformers and social scientists (Lady Wootton, for instance [1]) have taken this as evidence that the notion of responsibility, as assumed in English Law, is getting eroded. This does not necessarily mean punishment will also go, but it would end the last relics of the old retributive view that punishment is *deserved*. (Some philosophers have made the verbal point that in this case one should not speak of 'punishment' but only of, e.g., 'corrective treatment'.) The question would be simply what kind of 'punishment' would be likely to be effective as treatment, as reformative for the person, or as deterrent from the point of view of society. Notions of praise and blame would be disentangled from notions of deserts, and given when it is thought they would be effective in influencing conduct.[2] This way of thinking can appeal to 'learning theory', where a form of behaviour is seen as the cumulative result of a series of positive and negative reinforcements. Underlying this is the view that human nature is malleable to such conditioning. A difficulty in this view of 'punishment' is that prognosis of the effectiveness of treatment may be very uncertain, so that there would have to be an increase in indeterminate sentences. Would it therefore run up against a sense of injustice if very different sentences were given for similar offences? And would this influence their effectiveness? This may not be an insuperable objection; it does, however, show that each way of looking on the ethics of punishment has its difficulties. For if we abandon the notion that praise and blame should be earned by conduct which could have been otherwise, the notion of *corrective justice* (though not necessarily distributive

[1] See her *Crime and the Criminal Law* (Hamlyn Lectures, London, 1963). Lady Wootton points out that her views need not imply determinism; they are formed from a view of the purpose of criminal law and after seeing how difficult it is for the courts to decide on degrees of guilt and responsibility.

[2] Professor Nowell Smith has argued this point of view in his *Ethics* (Pelican Books, 1954), pp. 300 ff.

I

justice) would have to be abandoned. In this case we would have to say that the legal notion of a person as responsible, in the sense of answerable for an action, may be partly, if not entirely, a useful fiction related to actions in institutional settings. It may not correlate with whether or not the action was strictly the person's 'fault'. In any case 'He could have done otherwise if he had tried' is an unverifiable counter-factual. So if we are not happy about thus discarding the notion of responsibility in a non-fictional sense, the case for it has to be made, if it can be made, not on a hypothetical counter-factual but on categorical statements like 'I can do otherwise' said by an agent.[1]

We come again, as in the case of predictions, to the difference between an action from the point of view of an agent and of a spectator. It is possible for an observer to find causes and conditions pointing to the action; so can the agent when he looks back as an observer on his own action. Need such understanding foreclose the possibility of self-direction in the actual moment of decision? It need not do so, if knowledge of his own psychological make-up can give a person better control over it. A psychologist may say 'This explains why he acted as he did'. The agent may say 'This explains why I acted as I did; now I can take myself in hand'. Thus, as in prediction, the agent can be one move ahead of the observer, acting in the light of the information the observer gives him or that he himself acquires. This is assumed in psycho-analytic therapy; as Spinoza saw in his own way, understanding passions can lead to their mastery.[2]

---

[1] Cf. J. L. Austin, 'Ifs and Cans', *Proceedings of the British Academy* (1956), vol. XLII, and *Philosophical Papers* (Oxford, 1961).

[2] Cf. Stuart Hampshire, *Spinoza* (Pelican Books, 1951), on analogies between Spinoza's Ethics and psycho-analytic theory. Spinoza is sometimes accounted a determinist; but is control through understanding parallel to efficient causation through, e.g., desires? (I do not want to suggest that we are only free when our past behaviour has

'Self-control' is thus perhaps a less mystifying notion than 'free will' (though, intuitively, the latter is very likely an indispensable expression). By self-control is here meant a person's capacity not only to inhibit certain emotional reactions, but also to turn his efforts in one direction rather than another, to reflect critically on his 'goals', and on priorities among the things he wants. It can also mean that he can detach himself from thinking that the fact that he himself wants something is always a sufficient reason for giving it priority over what other people want — the kind of impersonality which is involved in the rationality of moral judgments. This self-control is, I think, more plausibly seen as a capacity of the whole person, as an organized system become conscious and capable of foresight, to orientate himself and direct his energies one way rather than another, than it is seen as the effects of acts of a separate spirit or mind somewhere behind the brain pulling the wires. That an intelligent organized system has these capacities is, no doubt, something which at present at least we cannot prove or explain. My own view is that the experience of using these capacities is less dubious than attempts to show that they do not exist.

At the same time, the capacities are not capacities to do anything whatsoever. The physical and psychological characteristics of our own kind of system are necessary if not sufficient conditions for what we can do. So also are some of the relationships which form our social environment. Psychological knowledge of people and their problems can show not what they must do, but the possibilities open to them with the equipment they have got. Even then, they may sometimes surprise us ('I didn't know he had it in him'). But what we call 'will power'

been explained to us and we act in the light of the information; I am saying that if we can do this, psycho-analysis is not deterministic as therapy. A person may also of course refuse to accept the information and go on as before.)

seems to be a matter of degree. Particularly, for instance, in work with retarded children one can learn to appreciate little victories and not be surprised by a lot of defeats. Often too a person's 'will', as capacity for concentration and control, can be strengthened by somebody else stiffening him; for there are educative and liberating as well as restrictive kinds of pressure (Alcoholics Anonymous might provide examples).

Such are ways in which psychological understanding increases rather than diminishes possibilities of freedom, through enlarging self-knowledge. We probably ought not to worry too much about the frontiers of responsibility in an absolute sense. Legally and socially, the frontiers can be fixed as answerability, but this may be partly an institutional convention. We can probably never say exactly where responsibility begins and ends in an internal, as distinct from this external institutional sense. Can we ever say just how much we owe to other people's stiffening and other people's encouragement? This is where Professor Maclagan's insistence, in his book, *The Theological Frontier of Ethics*,[1] that for an act to be moral one must be able to say 'It was all my own act', seems artificial. We are too much members one of another to be able to detect just where other people's influence ends and our own efforts begin. Yet the possibility of self-controlled and intelligently directed action, within limits, may not be a fiction. And psychological understanding may help to extend the limits.

It can of course be used not to extend them. Psychological knowledge can be used to 'manipulate' people: that is to say, to get them where you want them without their understanding and accepting the means by which this is being done, as in techniques of 'brainwashing'. Where do educational pressures turn into brainwashing? Perhaps the distinction is that in the former, the subject will be let

[1] London, 1961.

into the knowledge of what is being done, and the aim in the end is to release the pressures and let him act for himself.[1]   Again, we are brought to the liberating effect of *understanding*.   Examples of this effect, under actual experiences of 'brainwashing', are given in Dr. Bettelheim's *The Informed Heart*,[2] and in a pamphlet, *Creative Suffering*, by Julia de Beausobre.[3]   Both of these people were able to preserve their personalities against hysterical breakdown or the deadening of sensibility by achieving a detached interest in understanding what their interrogators were doing — Bettelheim by his professional interest as a psycho-analyst, Julia de Beausobre by an intuitive artistic and religious perception.

Can *sociological* understanding also show what possibilities are open, and enable us to enlarge our freedom by a clearer knowledge both of ourselves and of the situations in which we act?   Or is sociological understanding a form of explanation which shows how each action, given that situation, had to be as it was and not otherwise?

By 'explanation' I am meaning broadly any answer to a 'why' question which gives intellectual satisfaction.   This leaves open the possibility of different kinds of explanation according to the kinds of questions asked (psychological or historical, for instance, as well as sociological) and some explanations being better than others according to the criteria used.   R. B. Braithwaite [4] has said 'Any proper answer to a "Why" question may be said to be an explanation of a sort'.   So he holds the different kinds of explanation can best be appreciated by considering the different sorts of answers that are appropriate to the same or different 'Why'

---

[1] No doubt the first part of this distinction is not always possible in training children, but the second would still stand.   Cf. R. M. Hare, 'Adolescents into Adults' in *Aims in Education*, edited by T. H. B. Hollins (Manchester University Press, 1964).

[2] Free Press, Glencoe, Ill., 1960.   [3] London, A. and C. Black.

[4] *Scientific Explanation* (Cambridge, 1953), p. 319.

questions. In comment on this, Michael Scriven[1] has contended that sometimes explanations are replies to questions which begin, e.g., 'How could . . .' or 'What makes . . .'. I am not convinced that these could not be reworded as 'Why's' without too much strain. When he says some 'Why's' do not call for an explanation as answer, e.g. 'Why do you persist in lying?' where the reply is 'I have never lied about this affair', I should say that the reply claims that the question is improper, as based on a false assumption. I agree, however, with Mr. Scriven's main contention in this paper; that the model of explanation as deduction from general laws is only one way of justifying one type of explanation (this being, however, the most high-powered scientific kind),[2] and that different kinds of explanation can be adequate in context, i.e. in relation to what is already intelligible (not necessarily the same as 'familiar') to the person to whom it is made. So the explanation of the stain on the carpet being that I upset an ink bottle (Mr. Scriven's example) can be adequate in context, without needing reference to a general law, though there is of course the implicit *generalization* in the familiar fact that upset ink bottles cause stains (which is an empirical generalization rather than a law-like statement).

In some contexts, a teleological answer to a 'why' question may certainly give intellectual satisfaction. A general on a campaign may be able to make more sense of explaining his opponent's movements by asking 'What are they at?' than by asking 'What is impelling them to do this?'

[1] 'Explanations, Predictions and Laws', *Minnesota Studies in the Philosophy of Science* (1962), vol. III.

[2] Cf. R. B. Braithwaite, *Scientific Explanation*, especially Chapter IV. Robert Brown, in *Explanation in Social Science* (London, 1963), looks at different kinds of explanation; hypothetico-deductive theories; law-like statements connecting properties; explanations in terms of intentions, dispositions, habits, motives and reasons. There is an interesting review of Brown's book by I. C. Jarvie in *The British Journal for the Philosophy of Science*, vol. XV, no. 57, pp. 62–72.

In trying to understand human actions, it is sometimes helpful to give the kind of answer to 'Why are they doing this?' which allows actions may be purposive. It is also important to see the conditions which allow some purposes to be effective and others not and which give purposes room for manœuvre; and it is at least possible that to understand these conditions may lead those having the purposes to change some of them.

One concern of sociological explanations is with showing why some of the *results* of human actions are as they are because they take place in a social as well as a physical environment. In a social environment, each individual is set in multiple criss-crossing relationships, so that the results of his actions affect and are affected by those of other people, producing snowballing effects (such as inflationary spirals which no one has intended, though they can be understood and controlled through Keynesian economic techniques). Also the frameworks of actions are established patterns of social relationships and ways of doing things — institutions, in fact — which produce situations in which some kinds of action can be effective and other kinds discouraged or rendered ineffective. In a chaotic aggregate of individuals few purposes could be effective (the Hobbesian insight). Sociological analysis shows why some kinds of purpose are likely to be pursued effectively under some forms of social relationship and others not. Also, it shows how multiple social relationships produce reciprocating actions and reactions rather than single strands of cause and effect. So there will be consequential by-products which may frustrate an original purpose, or cause it to be achieved at a cost which, if it is understood, may make people ask whether the game is worth the candle. What is explained here is not the purpose, but why its consequences are as they are. Such diagnoses of consequences can be made in retrospect and explain why they were as they were, and this is one area of sociological explanation. It leaves open the possibility of modifying future action in the light of this information should similar situations recur.[1] The characteristically sociological part of such explanations consists in showing why some of the diagnosed consequences depend on multiple social relationships, and actions and reactions within these.

Sociological explanations can also be concerned with showing how certain features of people's behaviour are as they are because of their membership in social groups, and their positions in them, and the relations of these groups to others. Such actions in social relationships are not just like actions and reactions of physical bodies on each other. They take the form that they do partly because of the ways people see the alternatives before them; because of their expectations as to how others will act; and because of ideas as to what is required of them. So causality is here transmitted through people's minds, and explanations of behaviour will include psychological propositions about motives, about the envisagement of possible actions, and reasons for decisions. Such explanations will be *sociological* and not only psychological if they also contain propositions connecting these motives and reasons with how people find themselves in group relationships and their positions in these — predominantly, that is, with their roles. Yet to say someone has a certain role does not *explain* his behaviour unless it is being understood that he accepts this role so

1 This is not to say that all unanticipated consequences are simply due to ignorance and could be predicted and perhaps controlled by further knowledge. Some of them are like this; but the complexity of interrelated variables in social actions means that in practice full knowledge of their repercussions is often not possible. (Cf. R. K. Merton, 'The Unanticipated Consequences of Purposive Social Action', *American Sociological Review* (Dec., 1936), vol. I, no. 6.) Hence social policy making is most wisely pursued not on assumptions of omniscience, but by accepting the fact of what H. A. Simon calls 'bounded rationality'. (See below, p. 187.)

that it provides premises for his decisions.[1] There may be 'social pressures' on him to act as is expected in his role; but 'social pressures' are not physical forces; they are ways of providing people with strong motives for doing one thing rather than another. Durkheim and his immediate followers were right in insisting that sociological explanation should be given with reference to social groups and the relations between them.[2] They underestimated, even if they did not overlook, the fact that this does not do away with the need for some of the propositions in the explanation to be psychological propositions, since what is being shown is how membership and position in social groups provide motives for action and also limit what may or may not appear feasible or commendable.

Sociological understanding is concerned on the one hand with the interplay between impersonal causal and environmental factors, such as climate, food shortages (what Whitehead calls 'senseless agencies'[3]) and the interrelated sequences of effects produced by human actions; and on the other hand with the ways people try to manage their social relationships according to how they see their roles, and the rules of their established institutions. A sociological explanation will show why people behave in a certain way partly because of the exigencies of their environment, and partly because of how in their society they think it is appropriate to behave and how they see the possibilities open to them. This does not commit one to any particular view

[1] H. A. Simon, *Administrative Behaviour* (2nd edition, New York, 1957), p. xxx, interprets 'role' in this way.

[2] Cf. *The Rules of Sociological Method* (numerous editions), *passim*. Professor Homans, speaking of Durkheim's refusal to allow that social behaviour was also a product of individual consciousness, though not reducible to individual psychology, remarks 'To the classic peril of being impaled on the horns of a dilemma, we moderns should add a new one; being split on a false dichotomy'. *The Human Group*, p. 319. See also pp. 271 and 282; English edition (London, 1951).

[3] Cf. *Adventures of Ideas* (Cambridge 1933), pp. 6–7.

of the origins of these beliefs and motives. But it *is* concerned with how a person's place in a complex of roles may react on his beliefs and motives and serve to correct or reinforce them in unintended as well as intended ways. This is the point of the 'structural-functional' method, in so far as it is an explanatory and not only a descriptive method. Professor Kingsley Davis has said that 'functional method' is not the method of a particular school (still less should it be thought that there is a movement called 'Functionalism'). It is simply *sociological* method; but he goes on to say that functional statements in sociological analyses simply assert that certain phenomena have certain consequences.[1] In that case, I do not see how they can be *explanations*, unless either the consequences are looked on as intended, i.e. the explanation is teleological, or unless the consequences can be shown to react back on the activity, looked on not just as a single phenomenon but as a continuing process. Professor Merton has defined functional analysis in sociology as 'the practice of interpreting data by establishing their consequences for larger structures in which they are implicated'.[2] The functional view, that is to say, shows not just that something has consequences, but that it has consequences within a systematic complex of other factors and that it may contribute to the continuance of this complex by reinforcing the other factors. This need not be deliberately intended; it can happen when incentives for pursuing one activity, e.g. raising a family, serve to

[1] 'The Myth of Functional Analysis as a special method in Sociology and Anthropology', *American Sociological Review*, 1959, vol. 24.

[2] 'Manifest and Latent Functions' in *Social Theory and Social Structure* (revised edition, 1957), pp. 29 ff. See also my *Function, Purpose and Powers*, Chapter IV, for a fuller discussion than I can give here, though I do not think I quite saw the difficulty over *explanation*. I have taken this further in an article, 'Functionalism in Sociology', in *The Encyclopedia of Philosophy* (forthcoming; Crowell-Collier Publishing Co.; Free Press, Glencoe, Ill.; Macmillan Co., New York).

reinforce incentives for pursuing another, e.g. doing a job. This need not mean that someone is only interested in the job as a means of earning money to support his family, though in some cases it may mean this. Rather, it may mean the mutual reinforcement of motives, which I noted as the most plausible interpretation of Weber's thesis of the connection between Puritan religion and Capitalist economic enterprise.[1] Note that the 'function' becomes causally efficacious through reinforcing *motives*; possibly their insistence on eschewing any element of psychological causation in their sociological analyses has prevented some functionalists, such as Radcliffe Brown, from seeing this. Professor Nagel[2] has set out the conditions on which 'functional analyses' can produce causal explanations of, e.g., why a custom persists. Some of the consequences of a cause must react back on itself, and produce a corrective or reinforcement. Such analyses can be used in describing self-maintaining or self-regulating systems with 'feed-back'. Nagel holds that the relations between the elements in a system which allow this feed-back ought to be precisely specified; that very few 'functional analyses' in sociology exactly meet these requirements, and so that they tend to be descriptive rather than explanatory.

I think this is too harsh; it results from emphasizing the 'functional' aspect of sociological analyses, whereas the

[1] See above, pp. 91–92. In the short run this mutual reinforcement produced a distinctive way of life. In the long run, however, the consequences of the accumulation of wealth by ascetically minded business men made for an erosion of asceticism. This is an example of how unanticipated consequences are likely to react back and destroy a particular value under conditions where people pursue the value wholeheartedly without thinking about what these may be. R. K. Merton in 'The Unanticipated Consequences of Purposive Social Action' cites this as an instance of the kind of conditions which make an ideal self-defeating.

[2] 'A Formalization of Functionalism' in *Logic without Metaphysics* (New York, 1956).

characteristic sociological method is not just 'functional analysis'; it is *structural-functional*, and in this combination it is the structural part of the partnership which is more likely to be the explanatory part, while the functional part is more likely to be heuristic. I have already outlined what is meant by a structural explanation; it is an explanation which connects reasons for behaviour with membership of social groups related to other groups, and with people's position within these. This calls for psychological propositions about motives and premises for action, but psychological propositions where these are in terms of requirements and expectations in social relationships, so that the answer to 'why' is given by citing a structural fact. An example is Professor Merton's hypothesis about *anomie*. *Anomie* was the name Durkheim gave to a condition of moral restlessness, an inability to see or accept the norms of any clearly articulated social morality. Merton's hypothesis explains one source of this state of mind as due to a discrepancy between culturally accepted criteria of success along with social pressures to attain these, and the actual opportunities for attaining them. This can work both ways. There can be a generally accepted theory that one ought to get on in a hierarchical society, and yet for some groups there may in fact be limited social mobility. Or there can be mobility where those who move up are not in fact expected to do so, or socially recognized in the groups which they enter.[1] I am not here concerned with the truth or falsity of this view. The point is that it is a testable hypothesis for explaining the social behaviour described as *anomic*, and that some of its propositions relate to structural conditions of group relations in a society.

The functional approach by itself is heuristic; it says: 'Look for consequences of a custom or practice in some larger context'. If it can be shown that a consequence of the pursuit of one activity is to reinforce another activity,

[1] Cf. R. K. Merton, *Social Theory and Social Structure*, 2nd edition, Chapter V, especially pp. 190 ff.

this is heuristic in pointing to a problem for which the socio-logist may seek a structural explanation. If, for example, a requirement for taking part in religious ritual is that the participants be reconciled and in charity with each other, this may well strengthen their ability to co-operate in other joint enterprises. This does not explain why the ritual is per-formed. But we can then ask why it has this result, and see that a necessary condition is that the people concerned must be a group who like to do, or who have to do, things together in a number of contexts besides the religious one, as distinct from a society where people can attend rituals as solitary individuals without having to meet their fellow par-ticipants in other contexts. Also there may be rituals such as the 'Rituals of Rebellion' described by Professor Max Gluckman,[1] where the strengthening of social bonds comes from a symbolic acting out of conflicts in social relations out-side the ritual, such as the conflicts between authority and those subject to it, conflicts of sex, and of different age groups. Again, this is only an effective catharsis in condi-tions where, from choice or from necessity, there is an under-lying will to maintain these relations in spite of tensions; the ritual rebellion, as Professor Gluckman says, is not a revolu-tion. If a consequence of people joining together in the ritual is to help them to co-operate in other activities, it may turn out that their co-operation in these other activities strengthens their readiness to take part in the ritual, so that there can be a reaction back, making one reason why the practice is likely to persist (it may, however, only be a reinforcing reason; a phenomenon may indeed be 'over-determined' in that there is more than one sufficient con-dition present for its happening). What is shown in an 'explanation' of this kind is that certain structural con-ditions in the society account for some features at least of the ritual being as they are, and for some of its conse-

[1] *Rituals of Rebellion in South-East Africa* (The Frazer Lecture for 1952); Manchester University Press.

quences. In the ritual of rebellion, the parts of the participants may symbolize, either by correspondence or reversal,
their roles in the society beyond. If the ritual produces
'catharsis', this can be explained partly at least by showing
how taking part in it in these symbolic roles can provide a
way of facing tensions in the society beyond. Drawing on
Dr. Hilda Kuper's description of the Swazi Kingship cere-
monies, Professor Gluckman writes [1] 'One can feel the
acting out of the powerful tensions which make up national
life — king and state against people, and people against
king and state; king allied with commoners against his rival
brother-princes, commoners allied with princes against the
king; the relation of the king to his mother and his own
queens; and the nation united against internal enemies and
external foes, and in a struggle for a living with nature. This
ceremony is not a simple mass assertion of unity, but a stress-
ing of conflict, a statement of rebellion and rivalry against
the king, with periodical affirmations of unity with the king,
and the drawing of power from the king.'

Structural factors can also be invoked to explain what
kinds of people are likely to be 'joking partners', that is,
allowed licensed familiarity in *risqué* remarks and mock-
hostile behaviour. These are found to be people who are
neither members of an immediate 'in-group' nor of quite
separate groups. They occupy border-line positions, such
as the maternal uncle in a patrilineal family, and certain
clans which pair with others as joking partners. The
suggested explanation is that people in such border-line
relations can indulge in joking behaviour without damage
to authority within the group; and, as coming from persons
not directly concerned in the problems of the group, the
joking behaviour provides means of expressing playful
aggression, and also, like satire, sometimes includes pointed
moral rebuke amid the banter. Professor Gluckman has
suggested that the court jester occupies a joking relation to

[1] *Op. cit.* pp. 18-19.

the king; he is looked on as a half-outsider of uncertain social status, and is given a particular licensed role in which he can mix moral comment with his fooling.[1]

I suggest therefore that explanations of this type ought to be described not as 'functional explanations', but always as 'structural-functional' ones, where the explanatory side is likely to be the structural one, while the functional side is heuristic in pointing to a problem to be explained (for example, 'If the ritual has the effect of strengthening social cohesion, why should this be so?').

Structural explanations can be genuine explanations, in that they can be answers to the question 'Why (something)?' which give intellectual satisfaction at this level of analysis, even if they do not rise to the level of general law theories from which lower level hypotheses can be deduced (the paradigm of scientific explanation in a developed theoretical science such as physics). They are not explanations whose criterion of intellectual satisfaction is simply intuitive common sense. They show correlations of a non-obvious kind between behaviour and forms of social relationship, so that the latter can be seen as conditioning factors of the former. Since social relationships operate through the ways they are seen in people's minds, such explanations will be psychological as well as sociological, so what I have said earlier in this chapter about how far psychological explanations need or need not imply determinism is applicable here.

Another example, to which R. K. Merton has drawn my attention, comes from the experience of social scientists in American Universities and colleges during the McCarthy period. In a survey carried out by Paul F. Lazarsfeld and Wagner Thielens [2] it was found that the higher the quality

[1] See *Politics, Law and Ritual in Tribal Society* (Blackwell, Oxford, 1965), pp. 97 ff.

[2] Paul F. Lazarsfeld and Wagner Thielens, Jr., *The Academic Mind: Social Scientists in a Time of Crisis* (New York, The Free Press, 1958), pp. 168–178, especially the diagram on p. 173.

of the institution, the more frequent the accusations of 'politically subversive' activities and affiliations. But it was also found that the higher the quality of the institution, the less frequently did these accusations develop into threats to the position or freedom of the teacher. In those of low quality, the difference between accusation and threat was a mere 3 per cent of the cases; in those of high quality it rose to 28 per cent. ('High' and 'low' were assessed by criteria such as the number of volumes in the library and their ratio to the number of students; the ratio of the budget to the number of students; the scholarly productivity of the Faculty.) If we then look for an explanation for why there were far more accusations, but proportionately far fewer threats in the higher quality colleges than in the lower quality ones, it might of course be possible to produce a hypothesis that the more highly intellectual people, presumably employed by the former, are more likely to be subversive or thought subversive. This would need testing, and would not account for the marked decrease in the proportion of those to whom the accusation constituted a threat to their position. The conclusion suggested by the authors of the survey is a structural one; in the higher quality colleges, the administration had more regard for the independence of mind of their faculty, were more prepared to absorb the attacks and to 'build a security wall for [the teacher] behind which he could do his professorial work'. The expectation on the part of the teachers that the administration would see their role as that of maintaining the autonomy and integrity of the institution reinforced their readiness to speak their minds and risk accusations. The relation between the two groups within the institution was such as mutually to reinforce certain kinds of behaviour in each of them.

The two main emphases in sociological explanations which I have brought out, the emphasis on explaining consequences, and the emphasis on explaining behaviour, can be correlated with what Professor Popper calls 'the logic of situations'.[1] One meaning of this is an interpretation of people's motives and behaviour in terms of how *they* (not we) might be expected to see a situation in view of the kind of knowledge and outlook they have, given their traditions and institutions. Another meaning is the way in which some actions will be feasible and others frustrated because of the institutional system in which they happen, producing repercussions of unintended consequences. The first of these meanings, it might be said, has always been good historical method. The second is distinctively the sociological contribution, although sociological interest is also of course directed to the 'logic of the situation' in the former sense.

The 'logic of situations' allows that people may be rational, or more or less rational. Rationality for all of us is related to the evidence at our disposal and to our dominant thought forms. We can allow that these can vary and can be critically improved without having to postulate a 'prelogical' primitive mentality. By laying bare the 'logic of a situation' in which people have acted in the past, and also the factors limiting effective action which they may or may not have seen, sociological understanding can improve the rationality of those who take it into account in trying to make decisions in similar situations on further occasions. This is parallel to the way in which an understanding of individual psychology when communicated to the subject can encourage him to be rational.[2]

[1] See his *The Open Society and its Enemies* (London, 1945), vol. II, Chapter XIV. I. C. Jarvie in *The Revolution in Anthropology* gives a fuller account of Popper's views. Unfortunately the well-taken criticisms of structural-functional methods in this book are distorted by a propensity to put them in their naïver forms, and also by a highly emotional attack on them as 'inductivist'. But structural-functional method is not just generalizing from facts; it is, to use Merton's term, a 'general orientation' with which facts are approached.

[2] See above, p. 120.

K

It will be noted that in speaking of sociological explanation as most characteristically structural explanation, I have accepted the view of sociology and anthropology by which these are primarily studies of the institutional sides of social life, and the effects of institutional structures on social actions. There can also be an 'ecological' approach, looking at people's ways of living in relation to their natural environment.[1] There is of course also the approach of 'cultural anthropology', where different cultures are described as characterized by different dominant characteristics, such as acquisitiveness or moderation. Ruth Benedict's *Patterns of Culture* is the best-known example of this approach. I should describe this as social psychology rather than sociology. In any case, it seems less mystifying as a form of explanation to try to show how certain patterns of, e.g., family and especially marital relations produce situations in which people are likely to be jealous, rather than to say that a society is characterized by its members having a jealous disposition; or that a competitive economic system encourages acquisitiveness, rather than saying the system has been produced because the society is 'the Acquisitive Society'.[2] This is not to say that people's characteristics are simply a product of the social system; rather, the sociological interest may lie in seeing how, e.g., a competitive system encourages acquisitiveness and the fact that people are acquisitive accentuates the competitiveness of the system. We need neither take the high moral line that people get the institutions they deserve, nor need we say they are only what their institutions make them.

Sociological explanation need not, therefore, be incompatible with some degree of individual responsibility. It may, however, have a good deal to tell us about the effectiveness of individual actions. While actions based on personal

[1] Cf. R. Redfield, *The Little Community* (Uppsala, 1955), on how these approaches might be complementary to each other.

[2] The title of a well-known book by R. H. Tawney.

decisions may make a considerable difference to the life of the individual concerned and those directly associated with him, whether or not they will affect trends in the wider society may depend on structural conditions, the kinds of internal and external changes going on, and the opportunities these provide. I shall return to this point later.[1] As in psychology, knowledge of conditions limiting effective performance may help us to surmount some (though never all) of them. This is why the social sciences in their application are sometimes called 'policy sciences'.[2] They can produce rationally controlled methods of understanding and observing social data (quite enough to be called 'scientific' if one is fussy about the term) as a means of informing policy. The 'social data' so understood can help a person to see limitations on the effectiveness in a given situation of some of the alternatives he might otherwise wish to pursue. They may also, through showing the individual as occupying a position in a network of multiple roles, specify some of the premises (in the form of commitments, expectations, obligations) which he will be likely to take into account in forming his decisions. When all this is said, as individuals we may still have some initiative and room for manœuvre, though perhaps not as much as we like to think.

[1] See below, p. 149.

[2] Cf. *The Policy Sciences: Recent Developments in Scope and Method*, ed. D. Lerner and H. D. Lasswell (Hoover Institute Study, Stanford, Cal., 1951). The title is taken to point to 'the need for understanding man and society for the sake of the basic problems of our time'. It is not of course implied that the social sciences are only undertaken with a practical interest, but it is implied that they can produce understanding which can aid (not determine) practical policies, i.e. that it should be possible to form policies in the light of it. But then it must be possible to form policies, and this is a purposive and not a deterministic notion.

CHAPTER SEVEN

ROLES AND THEIR MORALITY

So far we have been mainly trying to scotch red herrings; views based as I believe on misconceptions, which would preclude the relevance of ethics and sociology to one another, or which would produce relevance by absorbing ethics into the descriptive study of *mores*, or by leaving no room for personal moral decisions. We have accepted the 'autonomy of ethics' so far as it argues against this; we have not accepted it so far as it insulates moral thinking from taking account of empirical facts. Ethics and sociology are indeed distinct, but they meet in a world where moral decisions have to be made in *situations*. A 'situation' is not just a conjunction of circumstances, but a conjunction of circumstances including social relationships seen as a unity in reference to actual or prospective action or interests, or to the attitudes of human beings. So a situation can be 'embarrassing', 'compromising', 'desperate', 'encouraging', 'delicate'; and a person can be 'master of a situation' or 'in its throes'. How a situation is seen will depend partly on the means at our disposal for understanding the social relationships, as well as the physical circumstances, that comprise it. Indeed, even to say 'comprise it' can be misleading, if this means that situations come in packaged deals. How we bound a 'situation' is a matter of how we see these relationships, and how far we are prepared to extend their network. Thus if we can see a situation religiously, so that the people in it, including ourselves, are seen not only in relation to each other, but to God and to each other in God, the 'situation' and what is important and unimportant in it may appear very differently from the way it appears on a secular view. Even on a secular view there can be wider and narrower ways of seeing situations, and they can be ordered in relation to different points of reference. A situation must be bounded somehow, both by definition and as a matter of practical necessity. Some humanitarian people tell us that we are linked with everyone else in the world, and no doubt there is truth in this, both empirically and morally.[1] But if we had to work out what to do in every situation in the light of its implications for the whole world, could we in fact decide what to do in our more immediate relationships? This recalls the old problem of 'internal relations' in the Idealist Logic, where we are told everything is an element in an over-all system in which it makes a difference to everything else, and everything else to it. I have said that some sociological views read like the modern repository of the doctrine of internal relations. A Social System is seen as a nexus of relationships in which the relation of A to B is also a relation of B to A, and the relation of A to B affects their relations to C, D, E, and vice versa; and so on, and so on. Indeed, this is probably all quite true; but if we are to talk and act with any effectiveness, we cannot just say there is one big web of reciprocal and ramifying relationships. Nor do sociologists in fact say this, and it is not necessary, even if we admit interconnections, only to think of the world as one great system in which everything is related to everything else. There are direct and reciprocal relations, and there are relations of varying degrees of indirectness. Some would be so indirect that to get round to them would be more like a dialectical defence of a notion of 'internal relations' than production of evidence for anything that could remotely be called 'interaction'. Thus sociologists do not in fact study

[1] It raises its difficulties about 'action at a distance'. A small boy was found trying to hold his breath; he had just been to a missionary meeting where he had been told 'Every time you draw a breath, some-one in China dies'.

one vast over-all Social System; they see webs of relationships divided into subsidiary webs or patterns of special
relationships, or, to change the metaphor for one of Professor Fortes',[1] of overlapping 'fields', some of which may
be affecting others, but whose special internal properties
can be studied. The notion of a role refers to such a special
relationship, while a 'role-set' is the group of relationships
associated with a particular role. A 'role performance' is
the enactment of a relationship of a specified kind, and in
any given society there will be certain ways of enacting a
role considered appropriate (as we have already seen, the
notion of a role has a reference to a norm of behaviour built
into it). In a role one sees oneself in a situation in relation
to others who also have their parts in the situation. It is of
course a metaphor from the theatre where one plays a role
as a part in relation to other parts. Even a one-man performance takes account of relations to others not present by
evoking the social background of the person soliloquizing;
Ruth Draper was able to produce a strong verisimilitude of
a number of characters not physically present from the way
she acted the relation to them of the one character who was
physically present. In the drama of social action as described sociologically, the roles may be closer to the roles in
a morality play than to the parts in realistic theatre. The
personae are not imagined individuals, such as Hamlet or
Othello; they are individuals seen as illustrating *types*, more
multifarious no doubt and less stereotyped than the types
in a morality play, but none the less types. Hence in a
sociological account of a social structure (as a network of
roles), there is always an element of abstract generalization
which is not just realistic description; and there is therefore
the problem of the relation of the abstraction to the realities
from which it is drawn.

A sociological explanation can show interconnections of

[1] *The Dynamics of Clanship among the Tallensi* (London and New
York, 1945), pp. 61 ff.

social relations with the help of sociological notions such as
role-set. As I also said in the last chapter, these produce
causal explanations through showing how people's motives
are corrected and reinforced by how they see their social
position *vis-à-vis* others. 'Motive' is of course a psychological concept. I think a difficulty arises if we then put the
problem 'How do we relate psychological and sociological
concepts?' as though we had an interaction between the
concepts of one discipline and those of another, rather than
seeing how factors in the concrete situation described
through the concepts of one discipline may be as they are
partly because of other factors in the concrete situations
which will be described through the concepts of another.
Let us illustrate by a simple diagram.

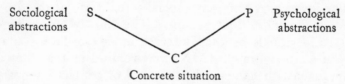

Concrete situation

What is going on among people in C may affect the
description of their psyches in the technicalities of P and
also the description of social fields or role-sets in S. But
the effect is via the happenings in C. P and S, as abstractions, do not interact with each other; to represent them as
doing so would be to commit what Whitehead called the
fallacy of misplaced concreteness. On the other hand, an
understanding of C as interpreted in P might lead a sociologist to revise his account in S; for instance, a psycho-
analytic view of a ritual might help him to see the social
alignments expressed in the ritual and described in S differently. But this would not mean that, e.g., 'The Uncon-
scious' would become a concept used in the presentation of
a Social Structure.[1]

[1] In *Closed Systems and Open Minds* (Edinburgh and London, 1964)
Ely Devons and Max Gluckman have discussed 'the limits of naïvety

Then what kind of abstraction is a Social Structure, and how is it related to actual happenings among actual individuals? I shall try to show how I see this with the help of the diagram on the next page.[1]

A diagram is of course a highly simplified and selective way of representing one or two of the relationships in a highly complex subject matter. If it succeeds in illustrating these, that is all that need be claimed for it. Of course a great deal more that is relevant to the problem will be left out, but if a diagram is too complicated it ceases to be useful as a visual aid. All this is very familiar; I am repeating it only because I know how grossly simplified the accompanying diagram is; all I hope is that it may help make its point, and it can then be discarded.

The lower part represents social actualities; at the tip, X, there is the individual person. The line MN represents actual individuals as they interact in face-to-face contacts (e.g. in a street brawl. 'MN' may remind us that they are individuals with names. In the kind of contact suggested, they may indeed be calling each other names.) OO' represents institutions, which are organizations in which people

in Social Anthropology', i.e. what line should a social anthropologist adopt when his research raises questions dealt with by other disciplines, such as economics or depth psychology. The authors suggest ways of distinguishing where 'naïve' assumptions about questions in these disciplines will not in fact affect the social anthropologist's analysis of his own problem, and where it is necessary to relegate the question as one requiring the techniques of an expert in the other discipline. They illustrate this from questions raised in a group of papers by colleagues published in the same volume. The discussion is relevant to the problem of 'internal relations' which I noted above: how does one circumscribe a field and what can be ignored?

[1] The diagram, its interpretation, and some of the subsequent discussion of it originally appeared in my paper 'How far can Structural Studies take account of Individuals?' in *The Journal of the Royal Anthropological Institute* (1960), vol. 90, part 2. It is reproduced here, with some modifications, with permission of the Editor.

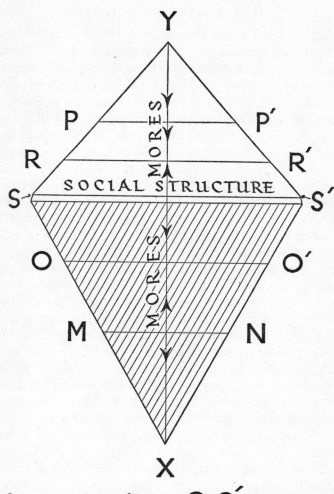

Y   Status as member of the Society

P P′ Descriptions of Social Situations

R R′ Institutions as patterns of roles

O O′ Institutions as Organizations

M N Individuals in face to face relations

X   Individual person

interact — a university for instance. Such an institution is an organization through which a succession of individuals passes. It is sometimes said that a Social Structure describes the form of a process through which individuals pass. But this will not do; even if a Social Structure is looked on dynamically, its elements are described as generalized roles. We therefore need this line OO′ to represent the inter- action of actual individuals in the actual institutional set- ting of organizations. Here we are still in the realm of actualities : an institution such as a University through its history, or a particular institution at a particular moment of time, such as Sir Alec Douglas-Home's Cabinet in 1964.

The upper half of the diagram shows the ways of talking about the actualities in the lower half, through which we approach to the abstract idea of the Social Structure, repre- sented by the line SS′ (it is a double line because we also approach it from below by observing the behaviour of the interacting individuals as represented on the lines OO′ and MN. But when we describe this behaviour, it will be in abstract terms represented in the upper half) . The apex Y stands for the individual considered in terms of his status as a member of the society. The line PP′ stands for descrip- tions of the face-to-face interactions at MN. We can call these accounts of social situations. In showing them as social situations, role terms will be used, e.g. 'neighbours', 'mother', 'policeman', and not simply individual names. Indeed the people represented on the line MN will probably be thinking of what they are doing in some such terms too, and the sociologist will observe them with certain role con- cepts already in mind, though he will also no doubt be adjusting the meaning of these by what he observes, and sometimes he may be seeing the need for a new role concept. So, though this may be description with very little analysis, it already uses classificatory words which are of course abstract words. RR′ stands for a still more abstract level, on which the institutions, which were actual organizations at an actual period of time in OO', get represented as patterns of roles — for instance, as in discussing the educational and social life of a university, or the office of Prime Minister in the Cabinet system. We can generalize these institutional patterns still further, and refer to, e.g., the governmental system of society, or its forms of education, and then we are passing to the idea of the Social Structure, represented by the top of line SS', which is the assemblage of the main recurrent institutional patterns in the society, seen as complexes of roles. (Of course in any actual analysis of any society, only the predominant patterns will in fact be able to be whittled out. So the term 'the Social Structure' is perhaps misleading, if it means that this is a unitary system, exhaustive of all the actual recurrent and important complexes of role behaviour in the society; new ones may at any time be being detected through observing behaviour in the actual contexts represented in the lower half of the diagram.) Since the lines in the upper half represent abstract ways of talking of the actualities in the lower half, I have made the diagram kite-shaped and not diamond-shaped, to indicate that if it is folded, the two triangular parts will not just coincide. In fact, of course, the actualities in the lower part are always infinitely richer and more complex than the ways of presenting them in the upper part. We can only describe and analyse at the cost of abstraction and simplification; nevertheless the descriptions in the upper part have to be drawn from and checked by observations of the actual behaviour in actual interactions indicated by the lower part.

There is also an especial way in which the existence of the individuals in the lower part must be taken into account in forming role concepts used in the upper part, a way which might be indicated by drawing a vertical line YX and calling it 'Social *Mores*'. This brings out the point that the abstract types are formed by generalizing from the behaviour expected as appropriate in the various roles they define. The types are idealizations, in that no one may behave just like this as a son or as a headman; but they define roughly how people think sons or headmen ought to behave, and this in a way not too far removed from how they usually do behave.

It is not accidental that the word 'institutions' appears in both halves. The canalizing of social interactions into institutions as actual organizations makes possible the abstractions of institutions seen as role patterns from which the notion of the Social Structure is derived. Moreover, institutions in both these senses depend on norms of expected behaviour, and so on *mores* and conventions. This is so whether the norms are highly formalized, as in the official procedures of a political system, or whether they are merely following tacit conventions, as in the unofficial arrangements of actual political life.

To return to our diagram. Looked at horizontally, from the point of view of theoretical analysis, the apex Y and the levels PP' and RR' thus represent abstract role patterns for the given society. But looked at vertically, in a way which could represent the point of view of the actual individuals at the apex X and on the levels MN and OO', acting in their various social capacities, these patterns are not just abstractions. They represent the very real claims and counter-claims which people's roles make upon them as they interact in actual social life. I have said 'counter-claims' advisedly, since these role obligations are not necessarily harmonious. Hence the difficulty of talking of 'the social system' as though it were unitary and coherent. There is of course an over-all status in membership of the society, and if we are considering a territorial society, there is an overriding legal system, and sometimes, though not always, a common political status of citizenship. At any rate everyone is within the bounds of law and government. Within this, there are constellations of roles, e.g. in family relations and in professional relations, and these are not necessarily coherent; in fact their obligations can and do conflict. So we can talk about 'a system' in the loose sense of an array of elements all of which are determined by some at least of the other elements. 'Array' here means more than a haphazard assemblage, because of common ties of legal status and membership of the society. But within this only some complexes of the role elements are linked with others; it is not a 'coherent' system in the sense of one in which the mutual determination of elements is complete, every role being related to every other role.[1] The expression 'the social system' should therefore be used with caution with this in mind; for this reason Fortes' notion of various superimposed social fields has much to recommend it.

The superimposition also happens in the lives of individuals. What, considered abstractly, is the superimposition of two fields, or role complexes, may appear to the individual as a painful choice between conflicting claims. A person finds himself in more than one constellation of roles, i.e. in 'multiple roles' and also in tensions between different claims within the same 'role-set'.[2] But in deciding what he ought to do, he will be likely to take into account, even if only to reject, notions of what is expected, e.g. of a son or of a headman. Social morality as well as custom, whether it comes to the individual as obligation or pressure to conform, or as occasion for rebellion and conflict, arises out of the possibility of making distinctions intuitively which are represented theoretically at the different levels of our diagram. It is only in extreme Existentialist literature that people can live just as 'Outsiders' or pure individuals, with no interest but one of contempt for role morality, with no awareness of problems arising out of possible conflicts between their roles, and with no institutional loyalties. The

---

[1] Cf. S. F. Nadel, *The Theory of Social Structure* (London, 1957), pp. 97 ff.

[2] For 'role-set', see above, p. 140. On types of response to conflicts within role-sets, cf. R. K. Merton, 'The Role-Set: Problems in Sociological Theory', *The British Journal of Sociology* (June, 1957), vol. VIII.

notion of role reflects this complexity in human moral consciousness and in the ways in which people see their social demands, as well as indicating the possibility of abstracting a regular pattern of social interaction.

So I have put arrows pointing upwards and downwards along the line YX; upwards to indicate that it is the existence of the *mores* (in a broad sense which includes convention as well as morality) which makes it possible to construct the concepts of role types needed on the levels PP', RR' and SS'; and downwards to indicate that the *mores* impinge in the form of obligations on the actual individuals on level MN and finally on the solitary person X. Thus in using these type concepts we are not just manipulating abstractions, as conventions with the help of which we can construct a pattern of a Social Structure. If our type concepts are appropriate and not obsolete, we are also talking about relations which can come home in practice to the actual individuals of the society in the form of obligations.

Sometimes changes in circumstances, and sometimes new ways in which some dominant individual plays a role, will establish a new pattern, and make it necessary to form a concept of a new role type, or give a different content to the old one. These are the lines, as it seems to me, on which structural studies can take account of change. The description of the Social Structure at any one time is of course a fixing of it at that time. But a structural account fixing a later stage can be set in juxtaposition with this, showing:

(*a*) that concepts specifying new role types are called for (e.g. the contemporary working-class 'Mum'); or,

(*b*) that a new distribution of roles has occurred (e.g. joint conjugal roles in contemporary married life); or,

(*c*) that the content of a role has changed (e.g. the British monarchy in the middle twentieth century, as a devoted family in the service of the nation).

Juxtapositions of structural accounts of the society at succeeding periods, showing that different role types are needed to describe the structure at period B from those needed at period A, are of course still only descriptions and not explanations of how the transition from A to B has come about. How far, in considering explanations for such changes, should account be taken of individuals? Sometimes some dominant individual may establish a new pattern. I doubt whether 'great men' or exceptional individuals are sociologically, as distinct from historically or psychologically, interesting unless they create a new role or change the image of an existing one, as Florence Nightingale for instance created the role of the trained professional nurse. Success in creating a new role may depend not only on the initiative and force of character of the pioneer, but on structural conditions in the society. Probably it would not have been possible to create the role of the trained professional nurse in a society where practically all the women married young, though now the role is established it is possible for there to be married women nurses — and also to break away from some of the austerity of the Nightingale tradition. It was important that at the time there was a supply of able, unmarried, idealistic young women for Florence Nightingale to recruit. Also the horrors of the conditions in the hospitals of Scutari made official opinion (reluctantly) prepared for the step. Yet the pioneer work might have ended with the emergency but for persistent efforts to go on and find institutional recognition of a new professional role. Other instances would be Dr. Arnold's reform of the Public Schools, and Dr. Jowett's reform of the tutorial system at Balliol College, Oxford.

It may be possible now to study an institution structurally without paying attention to the individual founder or reformer who has left his mark on it, but if we are looking for explanations of change, it is probably in the end not possible to leave him out. This is not to slip back from looking for social causes to looking for causes just in individual actions or to subscribe to a 'cult of personality'; it is to acknowledge what we all surely really believe, that an able person can make a difference by the way he uses opportunities provided by the external social changes affecting his particular community, particularly if it is one in which internal changes are going on too.

So in accounting for the difference between the Oxford tutorial system as Gibbon described it in his *Autobiography* and as it became after Jowett, we can take into account the demand for liberally educated young men in public life and in the Civil Service, and the effects of the Royal Commission of 1871 on the Universities. These were relevant social reasons for the reform of teaching, but they operated also on Cambridge where the reaction was different. Oxford produced pre-eminently the type of the amateur scholar interested in public life; Cambridge the professional specialist. The difference is perhaps less apparent now than a generation ago, and if so this is evidence for a tendency of structural and cultural factors to iron out particular differences in institutions made by particular individuals, if we take into consideration a long enough period. But in so far as there is still a difference, it is relevant to discuss whether it should be ascribed partly at least to Jowett's concern to make the tutorial system, and above all the Greats[1] school, into an instrument for educating young men with an eye to sending them out into influential jobs in the world. Cambridge, for better or worse, had neither the instrument of a Greats school, nor a Jowett, and it was perhaps more interested in fundamental thinking.

That I have said 'a Jowett' is significant. What we look for in drawing this kind of comparison between

[1] The Honour School of *Literae Humaniores* in classics, ancient history and philosophy.

societies is an individual with analogous qualities in an analogous position, achieving a comparable result appropriate to the different conditions of a different community. In other words, 'Jowett' is here not just the name of an individual, but in speaking of 'a Jowett' we are producing a role type (though certainly of only a low degree of generality). So if we ask how individuals enter into an account of a society, which is concerned not with historical narrative but with structural analysis, I suggest that this can be either through themselves being treated as role types of a low degree of generality; or through their being used as case studies illustrating the application of a role type of higher generality. We use these type concepts to exhibit relations between roles as institutionalized activities in a simplified picture of the society at a given time. Yet it is important to remember that the type itself is not a timeless essence, but it is used as a generalized concept for a pattern of routine behaviour in space and time in a given society, guided by normative expectations. This pattern is itself subject to change because it comes out of an historical process of interactions between individuals, but it is sufficiently regular over a period to be whittled out and fixed for theoretical purposes under the concept of a role type, though we have to be on the look-out for when this needs to be superseded. I do not think any general formal rules can be given for deciding where a type is no longer adequate to a changed pattern. This is a matter for skill in realistic observation on the one hand and powers of theoretical definition on the other. An instance of where a new role type seems called for would be found in the difficulty of adapting existing concepts of kinship as used by anthropologists to contemporary working-class family relationships. Studies of these by M. Young and P. Willmott [1] are cramped, I think, by trying to make the kinship concept

[1] *Family and Kinship in East London* (London, 1957). (I owe this illustration to A. E. Wilson.)

stretch too far to cover very loose relationships in the 'extended family'.

I have mentioned Existentialist literature as a dissentient voice. An Existentialist will see role morality as conforming to an expected type and being guided by rules, and so as sub-personal '*mauvaise foi*'. The metaphor of 'play-acting' can also be invoked, and the dead metaphor in 'hypocrite' revived; it may be said that a person is not acting from his own deep and individual powers of self-expression or responsible decision, but is thinking of how other people see him. This is put very forcibly by Sartre.[1] To accept a role is to evade the responsibility of seeing that one is free not so to act, and of freely deciding what one wants to be. It is to evade freedom by sheltering behind one's social function. This freedom Sartre calls 'contingency': the terrifying realization that there is no need to play this role, or indeed any other in particular, unless one so chooses. He writes [2] 'Among the thousands of ways, which the for-itself has of trying to wrench itself away from its original contingency, there is one which consists in trying to make itself recognized by the other as an existence by right. We insist on our individual rights only within the compass of a vast project which would tend to confer existence on us in terms of the function which we fulfil. This is the reason why man tries so often to identify himself with his function and seeks to see in himself only the "Presiding Judge of the Court of Appeal", the "Chief Treasurer and Paymaster", etc. Each of these functions has its existence justified by its end. To be identified with one of them is to take one's own existence as saved from contingency.' Sartre has dramatized this in his account of the café waiter.[3]

'Let us consider this waiter in the café. His movement

---

[1] See *L'Etre et le Néant*. English translation by Hazel E. Barnes, *Being and Nothingness* (London, 1957). The passages from this translation are quoted by permission of Methuen and Co. and Gallimard (Paris).   [2] *Op. cit.* p. 485.   [3] *Ibid.* p. 59.

is quick and forward, a little too precise, a little too rapid. He comes toward the patrons with a step a little too quick. He bends forward a little too eagerly; his voice, his eyes express an interest a little too solicitous for the order of the customer. Finally there he returns, trying to imitate in his walk the inflexible stiffness of some kind of automaton while carrying his tray with the recklessness of a tight-rope-walker by putting it in a perpetually unstable, perpetually broken equilibrium which he perpetually re-establishes by a light movement of the arm and hand. All his behaviour seems to us a game. He applies himself to chaining his movements as if they were mechanisms, the one regulating the other; his gestures and even his voice seem to be mechanisms; he gives himself the quickness and pitiless rapidity of things. He is playing, he is amusing himself. But what is he playing? We need not watch long before we can explain it: he is playing *at being* a waiter in a café. . . . This obligation is not different from that which is imposed on all tradesmen. Their condition is wholly one of ceremony; the public demands of them that they realize it as a ceremony. There is the dance of the grocer, of the tailor, of the auctioneer, by which they endeavour to persuade their clientèle that they are nothing but a grocer, an auctioneer, a tailor. A grocer who dreams is offensive to the buyer, because such a grocer is not wholly a grocer. Society demands that he limit himself to his function as a grocer, just as the soldier at attention makes himself into a soldier-thing.'

Of course the role of a waiter is a particularly stylized one. George Orwell noted this in *Down and Out in Paris and London*.[1] 'It is an instructive sight to see a waiter going into a hotel dining-room. As he passes the door a sudden change comes over him. The set of his shoulders alters;

[1] P. 68 (2nd edition, London, 1949). Quoted by courtesy of Martin Secker and Warburg, and of Harcourt Brace and World Inc., by permission of Brandt and Brandt.

all the dirt and hurry and irritation have dropped off in an instant. He glides over the carpet, with a solemn priest-like air. I remember our assistant *maître d'hôtel*, a fiery Italian, pausing at the dining-room door to address an apprentice who had broken a bottle of wine. Shaking his fist above his head he yelled (luckily the door was more or less soundproof):

"*Tu me fais* — Do you call yourself a waiter, you young bastard? You a waiter! You're not fit to scrub floors in the brothel your mother came from. *Maquereau!*"

'Words failing him, he turned to the door; and as he opened it, he delivered a final insult in the same manner as Squire Western in *Tom Jones*.

'Then he entered the dining-room and sailed across it dish in hand, graceful as a swan. Ten seconds later he was bowing reverently to a customer. And you could not help thinking, as you saw him bow and smile, with that benign smile of the trained waiter, that the customer was put to shame by having such an aristocrat to serve him.'

The Existentialist has his point. There is a real tempta-tion to seek security in having a function, especially if it is one that carries 'status' (in the colloquial prestige sense, not the sociological sense, where a status is simply any position in a social structure). But is it not possible to take role and function seriously without absorbing the person in the *persona*? (We shall return to this.) And is Sartre right in saying that 'society demands that a grocer limit himself to his function as a grocer'? There is indeed an epitaph on a tombstone in a Scottish burial-ground which reads 'Here lies the body of Tammas Jones, who was born a man and died a grocer'.[1] But 'society' in general is an abstraction. It can be broken down into numbers of people some of whom meet the grocer *qua* grocer in the role of his

[1] Quoted by W. L. Sperry, *The Ethical Basis of Medical Practice* (London, 1951), p. 41.

customers, others of whom meet him as fellow members of his local church council or bowling club, others as members of his family and his friends. Sartre speaks as if there was one role with which a person can identify himself. In fact 'one man in his time plays many parts', and these not only successive ones.[1] Their obligations may pull him in different directions, and he has to find his own way of dealing with such conflicts. The fact that *different* roles and their obligations press upon the same person makes it impossible to think of him realistically as simply the incumbent of a role, though abstractly he can be so thought of as an element in a Social Structure.

Yet the Existentialist still has a point. It is possible for those who deal with grocers to forget that they are also human beings; hence the need for the protective regulations of Shop Acts, Early Closing Days and the like. Are we left then with an antithesis between role behaviour on the one hand with its legal and moral regulations, which Sartre says evades the full freedom and responsibility of the individual, and on the other hand, a purely personal morality, free, spontaneous, unbound by rules?

The trouble about this antithesis is that it hardly comes to grips with social morality, and whether we like it or not, social morality impinges on our lives most of the time. We had much better recognize and respect the fact that, as Aristotle remarked, he that could live apart from society might be a beast or a god, but not a human being. (Solitary hermits have not been born such; they are also visited occasionally, and they relate themselves to God and the world in prayer.) To live in society means, we have seen, that a certain number of reasonably stable functions and expectations can be depended on. There may be a variety of 'reference groups' in any given society, a choice of the groups whose standards one respects, or in whose eyes one

[1] As in Jaques' speech: *As You Like It*, Act II, Sc. VII, ll. 139–166.

wants to be in good standing.[1] Those who most want to assert their freedom to be a law to themselves and to contract out of established society — Outsiders, Beats or their *avant-garde* successors — soon begin to produce their own codes defining what is in and what is out in their circles. Feiffer in some of his cartoons has satirized the anguish of the Beat who is uncertain where he stands in his nonconformist conformity. We probably all need approval and support from some people at least some of the time. There may be occasions on a specific issue when there is *Athanasius contra mundum*, but not all the time, or all along the line. It looks also as if Athanasius must have mustered considerable support; why else the Athanasian Creed? The person who makes a stand on a specific issue is more likely to be effective if he is not known as a professional objector. We all know the stage army of the good, who are brought in to sign protests on every possible issue, and no doubt they form a reference group of great solidarity among themselves.

Both role behaviour and the mutual support of people for one another in their reference groups thus go deep into our everyday lives, and do not merely provide useful abstractions for sociological theory. They may even be bound up with our own awareness of ourselves as agents. At least this was the view of G. H. Mead, who was probably responsible for introducing the notion of 'role' in its sociological sense.[2] The development of self-consciousness,

[1] A 'reference group' need not be a group to which a person actually belongs. It may be one to which he aspires to belong, or on whose ways he models his behaviour by 'anticipatory socialization'. There is not always an obvious answer to the question 'Who are the Joneses?' There is a full discussion of a number of aspects of this by R. K. Merton, 'Contributions to the theory of Reference Group Behaviour' (Chapter VIII in *Social Theory and Social Structure*. Revised edition, 1957).

[2] Cf. *Mind, Self and Society*, edited by C. H. Morris (Chicago, 1934). The highly influential lectures out of which this book was composed had been given from 1904 onwards.

according to Mead, comes through one's being able to call out responses in oneself as well as in others. So comes a realization of others as related to oneself and oneself to others, and thus their attitudes become internalized in an attitude to oneself. Mead's view of the internalized attitude of a 'generalized Other' has obvious affinities with Freud's Super Ego, but it is less closely bound up with immediate emotional ties with the parents.[1] A person to Mead is built up out of internalized roles, so that 'the expectations of others have thus become the self-expectations of a self-steering person'.[2] Mead does not imply that an individual is nothing but a collection of roles: indeed he repudiates this. He does not deny that an individual may have his own style and character; what he underlines is that this exists and develops through relationships to others. In 'reflexive' role-taking a person learns to see himself through the attitudes of others and to enter imaginatively into their roles. This may produce a 'What will they say?' kind of conscience; it may also go on to become something more objective — the notion of how one might appear to someone not directly involved in the situation, in fact Adam Smith's 'impartial spectator'. This clearly links up with the notion of Universalizability, the possibility of judging what one ought to do in a given situation by not making an exception in one's own favour to what one would judge anyone else similarly placed ought to do. Sartre, indeed, with all his Existentialism, is Kantian enough to allow this. One may not always have a precedent to follow

---

[1] Talcott Parsons similarly, and explicitly, takes a broader view than Freud of the Super Ego, through seeing it as the internalizing of a wider range of social relationships. See 'The Super Ego and the Theory of Social Systems', in *Working Papers in the Theory of Action* (with R. F. Bales and E. A. Shils, New York, 1953).

[2] Gerth and Mills, *Character and Social Structure* (London, 1954), p. 84. This book develops Mead's initial view in terms of contemporary social psychology.

in making a decision, but one is creating a precedent; for in legislating for oneself, he says, one legislates for the whole world.

Role morality represents this impersonal element in morality. In a role one is a person of a certain kind put in a certain kind of relationship, and thus detached from purely personal idiosyncrasy. We shall be concerned later with whether a person can also achieve detachment from his roles; that is another story. Here we are concerned with the character of role morality. As a directive for behaviour in certain kinds of relationship, it is structured by rules; if not by explicit and sanctioned rules, at least by implicit understandings, and maxims, or rules of thumb, as to how such a person would behave in this kind of relationship.

The most articulate case of this, where the rules have been deliberately thought out, is a professional code. A profession, to quote Talcott Parsons, 'is a cluster of occupational roles, that is roles in which the incumbents perform certain functions valued in the society in general, and by these activities, typically earn a living at a full time job. Among occupational role types, the professional is distinguished largely by the independent trusteeship exercised by the incumbents of a class of such roles of an important part of the major cultural tradition of the society.'[1] A profession thus carries with it the notion of a standard of performance; it is not only a way of making a living, but one in which the practitioners have a fiduciary trust to maintain certain standards. These are partly standards of competence, or technical ability in carrying out 'functions valued in the

[1] *Essays in Sociological Theory*, revised edition (Free Press, Ill., 1954), p. 372. The papers 'A sociologist looks at the legal profession' and 'The Professions and Social Structure' in this volume are a full and interesting treatment of the notion of a professional role ; as is also Chapter X, 'The case of modern medical practice', in Talcott Parsons' *The Social System* (Tavistock Publications, London and New York, 1952).

society'. But not only so: professional competence has to be joined with professional integrity. The implications of this in a particular profession have been the concern of professional codes from the Hippocratic Oath (about the 4th century B.C.) onwards. A professional man carries out his function in relation to people who also stand in a particular role relation to him. The relationship carries specific obligations, to be distinguished from those of purely personal morality, or from general obligations to human beings as such.[1] It must be distinguished from these, but it may overlap with them, and in some cases this may produce acute moral problems. Because of these difficulties and potential conflicts, some of the older established professions, notably medicine and the law, have formulated principles of professional conduct to guide their practitioners, and violation of these can be matters of discipline within the profession itself. Conduct prescribed by a professional code encourages such confidence between the professional person and his client as will make it more likely that the function in which they are both interested will be carried out successfully. This is a clear case where a morality cannot be looked on as purely a matter of feeling or convention, since here at any rate it can be given a rational justification in terms of the requirements of the job. An instance is the obligation on doctors and lawyers not to divulge confidential information about their clients' affairs to third parties. The assurance that communications will be respected is necessary to establish confidence between the practitioner and his client. But this confidential relationship has to be distinguished from personal intimacy, in the general as well as

[1] In this passage and those following, I am drawing, with the Editor's permission, on an article 'The Notion of a Professional Code' which I contributed to *Crucible*, Oct. 1962, a Quarterly Review, published by the Church Assembly Board for Social Responsibility. This was followed in subsequent numbers by articles by professional men, discussing their own professional ethics.

in the particular euphemistic meaning of the term. Talcott Parsons says that a professional person has to be able to maintain 'affective neutrality'.[1]   A doctor may not be able to help *liking* some of his patients more and some less than others, but he must not let himself get into an emotional relationship with a patient.   Psycho-analysts in particular have had to give careful thought to the ethical restraints necessary in the 'transference' situation, where an emotional attitude on the patient's part has to be allowed temporarily for therapeutic reasons.   Studies of the medical student made in Columbia University found, however, that the physician is taught both the dominant norm of affective neutrality and the subsidiary norm of affectivity (the expression of compassion and concern for the patient). Hence they describe the physician's role as one involving *'detached concern'*, calling for alternation between the impersonality of detachment and the expression of compassionate concern.   Such apparently contradictory norms call for sensitivity to changes in the needs of the patient, in passing from one to the other; this is likely to produce ambivalence in the patient's attitude to his doctor, the patient not appreciating the reasons for detachment.[2]

An ancient instance of professional ethics is the 'seal of the confessional' whereby a priest is bound not to divulge what he hears from his penitents in confession.   In this case there are sacramental as well as ethical reasons, since the

[1] 'Affective neutrality' versus 'affectivity' is one of the contrasts in the table of five pattern variables Parsons distinguishes in drawing up a typology of orientations in different kinds of roles. Other contrasts are Particularism-Universalism;   Diffuseness-Specificity; Achievement-Ascription;   Collectivity-Self Orientation.   See T. Parsons and E. A. Shils, *Towards a General Theory of Action* (Harvard, 1951), p. 77.

[2] Cf. R. K. Merton and Elinor Barber, 'Sociological Ambivalence' in *Sociological Theory, Values, and Sociological Change* (New York, 1963).

priest is looked on as instrumental in the relation between
the penitent and God. These communications are not asked
for in a court of law, even if they are not technically 'privileged', i.e. immune from having to be disclosed under threat
of contempt of court on refusal, and priests everywhere
would no doubt hold that they ought to go to prison rather
than break the seal of the confessional. Communications
between lawyers and their clients are privileged. The reasons for this were given by Knight-Bruce L.J. (1846).
'Truth, like all other good things, may be loved unwisely —
may be pursued too keenly — may cost too much. And
surely the meanness and the mischief of prying into a man's
confidential consultations with his legal adviser, the general
evil of infusing reserve and dissimulation, uneasiness, suspicion and fear into those communications which must take
place, and which, unless in a condition of perfect security,
must take place uselessly or worse, are too great a price to
pay for truth itself.' [1] The relation between the professional
person and his client is, however, only one of the role relationships in which he is professionally concerned. His
'role-set' comprises also his relationships to his colleagues,
and his relations as a professional person to the lay public.
Thus, though a barrister is under an obligation not to
divulge communications between himself and his client, he
also has a duty to the court and to the cause of justice.
While his duty is to put the best interpretation he can on
the evidence in the interest of his client, he must not
deceive the court by making a statement he knows to be
false. Professional ethics as between colleagues are intended
as means of maintaining mutual trust and collaboration
within the profession. They normally prescribe that a professional person shall not advertise his services, shall not
entice clients from another practitioner, shall be ready to
help a colleague in case of need. Some of these matters are

[1] Pearse *v.* Pearse (1846): I De Gex and Sm. 28, 29. Quoted by
Quenton Edwards in 'The Law of Privilege', *Crucible* (Jan. 1964).

questions of 'professional etiquette'; the border-line between etiquette and ethics is, however, not easy to draw, as,
for instance, in the convention that a barrister only sees a
client in the presence of his solicitor and only accepts a brief
through a solicitor.[1]

A professional code can therefore be justified on functional
grounds, as promoting the kind of relationship within which
a job is most likely to be done effectively. But its importance
is not only functional; the behaviour becomes valued on its
own account as a matter of professional integrity, and adds
to the respect with which a professional person is regarded
in the community.[2] This does not mean, however, that
everything about professional codes is beyond criticism.
They are in the nature of the case pre-eminently conservative, in the literal sense as conserving the moral and intellectual tradition of the profession, and also in the sense of
being administered by what tends to be a conservative hierarchy, not always adaptable to new demands and new social
conditions. Moreover, it is an element in most professional
codes that individuals themselves should not advertise.
Thus the professional association which is the guardian of
the code will also be likely to be concerned with forwarding
the pecuniary interests of its members. And since professional people are generally interested, in a more or less
polite way, in being well paid, it is possible for the public to
be cynical about 'professional services'. Nevertheless, it is

---

[1] Cf. W. W. Boulton, 'A Guide to Conduct and Etiquette at the
Bar of England and Wales' (London, 1953).

[2] Cf. R. K. Merton, 'Some Thoughts on the Professions in
American Society', Brown University Papers, no. XXXVII, p. 9.
On the 'composite of social values that makes up the concept of a
profession' Merton lists 'first, the value placed upon systematic
knowledge and the intellect: knowing. Second, the value placed upon
technical skill and trained capacity: doing. And third, the value
placed upon putting this conjoint knowledge and skill to work in the
service of others: helping. It is these three values as fused in the
concept of a profession that enlist the respect of men.'

part of the notion of a profession that payment is for *services* in which the practitioner is concerned with the interests of his clients, and in some professions it is against the code to sue for unpaid fees. Socrates put the point long ago: 'This benefit, then, — the receipt of wages — does not come to a man from his special art. If we are to speak strictly, the physician, as such, produces health; the builder, a house; and then each, in his further capacity of wage-earner, gets his pay. Thus every art has its own function and benefits its proper subject' (*Republic*, 346 d). A profession combines both these 'arts', and the importance of the professions in our society shows that a simple distinction between self-interested and altruistic conduct cannot always be maintained. 'Professional conduct' is so designed as to make the motives of desire for success, of service to others and of personal integrity tend to point in the same direction. This may not be the deepest form of sacrificial morality; nor in a largely competitive society is it one to be despised.

I have said that a professional code is a matter of role morality, to be distinguished from a universal morality of person to person. It is concerned with how one should act in a certain capacity. Yet at the same time we esteem the doctor or teacher who also 'treats people as people' (i.e. with the 'concern' as well as the 'detachment'). This does not mean that the special restraints of the role can be abrogated by entering into a purely personal relation or by mixing one's roles. Thus, it can be part of a code that one should not use professional influence to get one's friend or relative a job where his claims may not be as strong as those of other candidates. This professional disapproval of 'nepotism' may be culture bound to Western society, in that in some other cultures it is said to be a first duty of anyone who gets into a position of influence to look out for the interest of his friends and relatives and fit them out with good jobs. This must surely produce real moral conflicts in the minds of new-comers to responsible positions in some of the newly developing countries. But if we say that the professional tradition against nepotism is culture bound, does this mean that it is purely a relativistic matter of historical development? Or are there good reasons against nepotism, reasons which are an application of the wider principle that one should not adjudicate on a matter in which one has an interest — or if one must do so one should declare one's interest? This in turn is part of the still wider principle that justice should not only be done, but be seen to be done.

This is only one of the ways in which personal demands of friendship and family may come into conflict with the demands of a role morality. The professional person will be subject to all sorts of pressures for time and attention as well as for favour. Here a professional code can help, for instance by enabling him to say that there are some things he is not at liberty to do. Such restrictions, while in one sense limiting his freedom, in another sense can safeguard it, in making it clear that there are some matters about which he is not open to argument.[1] Problems of role morality can also arise where there is a conflict of roles, e.g. that of scientific researcher and of medical practitioner. This is the subject of a code of ethics on experiments on human subjects, both in clinical research while they are undergoing professional treatment, and in non-therapeutic clinical research, which has recently been accepted by the World Medical Association.[2] In the former case, it is stated that 'the doctor can combine clinical research with professional

[1] Philip Selznick speaks of the 'exclusiveness' of professional groups as one of the factors which can help them to get 'that insulation from day to day pressures which permits new ideas and skills to mature', *Leadership in Administration* (New York, 1957), p. 121. Insulation from certain external pressures, that is to say; there will be plenty of pressures arising out of the work itself.

[2] The final draft, as accepted by the W.M.A. at Helsinki in June, 1964, and known as the 'Declaration of Helsinki', has been printed in full in the *British Medical Journal*, July 18th, 1964, with a supporting editorial.

care, the objective being the acquisition of new medical knowledge, only to the extent that clinical research is justified by its therapeutic value for the patient'. If at all possible the doctor should obtain the patient's freely given consent after full explanation. If this is not possible, on account of legal or physical incapacity, the consent of the legal guardian should be obtained. In the latter case, the nature, purpose and risk of clinical research must be explained to the subject, and his free consent obtained. It is also stated that in non-therapeutic research 'the subject of clinical research should be in such a mental, physical and legal state as to be able to exercise fully his power of choice', that at any time he should be free to withdraw permission, and that the investigator should discontinue the research if in his judgment it may prove harmful to the individual.

The code is explicitly based on the assumption that a human subject on whom experiments may be carried out is a *person* with reason and power of choice (a 'subject' indeed, and not an 'object' of experiment); or if, through legal or physical incapacity he cannot exercise these powers, his legal guardian must exercise them on his behalf. Thus, here in contrast with the idea that to apply science to human subjects involves regarding them deterministically, this ethical code for a certain area of scientific experiment is based on an assertion of their right to be treated as capable of rational and responsible decisions. In this way such a code, far from leading to a streamlined and inhuman way of looking on human subjects, can stress mutual responsibility within a professional relationship.

Yet, however much a professional code may give guidance on some matters, there will still be conflicts and pressures where a person is thrown back on his own moral resources, and where to see a solution may call for a high degree of intelligence. This has been well put by Chester Barnard in *The Functions of the Executive*,[1] bringing out the two aspects of

[1] (Harvard, 1938), p. 276.

ability and moral resource which are both required in order to meet such problems. 'While, on one hand, the requisite ability without an adequate complex of moralities or without a high sense of responsibility leads to the hopeless confusion of inconsistent expediencies so often described as "incompetence", on the other hand, the requisite morality and sense of responsibility without commensurate abilities leads to fatal indecision or emotional and impulsive decisions, with personal breakdown and ultimate destruction of the sense of responsibility. The important distinctions of rank lie in the fact that the higher the grade the more complex the *moralities* involved, and the more necessary higher abilities to discharge the responsibilities, that is, to resolve the moral conflicts implicit in the position.'

It is surely no evasion of the moral responsibility of the individual to ask that some lines may be laid down for his guidance in some of the more typically recurrent problems and temptations which he will meet in his professional roles. For it is abundantly clear that this will not mean that his own powers of moral judgment need go unexercised.

CHAPTER EIGHT

PERSONS AND PERSONAE

WE have considered role morality in its most articulate form: a professional code, where there can be little dispute both that the code is a form of morality, and that the profession is a role. Other instances may, however, be less clear. How far does the notion of role extend? Is every form of human relationship a role, and if so, has it some notion of appropriate behaviour associated with it ('appropriate' including etiquette and not only morality)? Even if the answer to the first question is yes (and I am not certain that it should be), the answer to the second is, surely, no. There are many relationships in which people are uncertain of how to behave (genuinely uncertain, and not only ignorant or boorish), and this need not only mean that they are uncertain of their role. We can, indeed, distinguish a number of degrees of structuring of role morality ('degrees' here standing for definiteness of articulation, and not necessarily for depth of human commitment). For instance, there are:

1. Legal obligations, officially specified, with sanctions.
2. Professional ethics, sometimes formalized and guarded by a body with disciplinary powers (e.g. medical ethics).
3. Professional ethics which are less formalized, and where there is no disciplinary body. (Social workers on the whole belong to this category; at least in Great Britain and America, where their professional code is often discussed in an unofficial way.)
4. Role morality for a clearly recognized status, e.g.

marriage and parenthood. (The *mores* may, of course, change but at least the status is reasonably clear.)

5. Role behaviour where status is uncertain, for instance, courting behaviour: in English colloquial parlance the status is clarified somewhat when someone becomes a 'steady'.

6. Role morality in human relationships which are very little defined, but which may be deep and exacting; for instance, friendships.

The notion of role is more obviously applicable to the first four of these than to the fifth and sixth, where we are more likely to want just to speak of 'personal relations'. By including them as forms of role morality, I suggest the notion is still operative, even if recessive. Is there a clear line to be drawn between role relations and personal relations?

Whether all social behaviour is behaviour in a role is surely partly a matter of terminology. Is it more useful to keep the term 'role' for the more recurrent, recognizable types of relationship? Or should we use it quite generally, so that even in a purely temporary relation, for instance where someone quickly catches hold of someone else who is slipping in getting off a bus, the former is in the role of a helper and the latter in that of a person being helped, so that an attitude of solicitude is appropriate on the one side and one of gratitude on the other? I exclude the case where the helper is the conductor, since it might plausibly be said that to do this kind of thing is part of what is expected from a person in his job. The helper should be a chance fellow passenger. The use of the word 'fellow' suggests that this can indeed be seen as a role relation with its appropriate courtesies and obligations. But what about unexpected and uncovenanted acts of kindness and consideration, imaginative and it seems spontaneous, which no one, it could be said, had the right to expect, and yet of which it could also be said that they were entirely appropriate? On the whole, to return to the question of terminology, it seems best to keep the notion of role to apply to relationships which are sufficiently structured to be classified under common names, which have some pattern of conduct associated with them, recognized in the breach as well as in the observance. Otherwise, if any form of social relation, however transitory or spontaneous, is to be a role relation, the concept will become so all-embracing as to lose its effectiveness as a tool of social analysis. It can thus be distinguished from relations of a quite transitory kind, and from spontaneous behaviour which is purely impulsive and idiosyncratic (if indeed there is any such). The latter may, of course, cover some of the most precious kinds of personal behaviour; but the fact that we have distinguished role relations from transitory social relations is significant. For this suggests that the more enduring forms of social relation, however deeply personal they may be, are also role relations. Our ordinary usage as well as common law recognizes this, in giving relations such as those of husband and wife a socially recognized status with specific rights and obligations.

I have said that whether or no all personal relations are also role relations is *partly* a matter of terminology; and in so far as it is, I have opted for reserving the term for those relations whose forms are sufficiently repeated to be classified under common names. But there is a substantive as well as a linguistic point at issue, which can be brought out by asking whether friendship is a role relation. It may be significant that we want to say both yes and no to this. Yes, on the verbal point that 'friend' is a recognized social category. No, on the score that we think every friendship is unique, a matter of spontaneity and mutual affection and not of rules. But we have already seen that we must distinguish the comparatively clear-cut notion of following rules such as the rules of a game from the diffuse notion of appropriate behaviour, where the guiding lines may be more or less indefinite, behaviour being a matter of 'knowing how' (in Ryle's phrase), rather than of following explicit directions; and role behaviour, we have seen, can admit of degrees of structuring. There is a further point. A role, as we saw in the last chapter, is a name for a typical relation in which typical action is expected. The role relation is an abstraction, called by a common name. In any concrete situation of relationship, we have not just an instance of the role, but a particular person enacting his role — what sociologists call a 'role performance'. In practice therefore we have to do with role performances, where the 'role' can answer to the generalizable, and so impersonal, aspect of the relation, and the 'performance' to the individual's own special style. In other words, we have to do with the person in the *persona* and the *personae* of the person. In the case of a highly personal relation such as friendship, the substantive as distinct from the verbal question is not so much whether or not one calls it a role as whether or not there should be an impersonal element even within a highly personal relation. Aristotle may not quite have said this when he said that every form of friendship has an appropriate form of justice associated with it,[1] but he gave a clue. Justice need not mean one stands on one's own rights (though sometimes it does mean this). It means recognizing that another person has his rights; that he should be respected as having thoughts, interests, perhaps a vocation of his own, and not only to be absorbed in romantic affection.[2] John Macmurray sees this, both in what he says about justice and in what he says about 'withdrawal and return', in his *Persons in Relation*.[3] He makes, however,

[1] *Nicomachean Ethics*, VIII, ix.
[2] C. S. Lewis, who could be perceptive about forms of human relation, brings this out in his treatment of friendship in *Four Kinds of Love* (London, 1960).
[3] The second volume of his Gifford Lectures, *The Form of the Personal* (London, 1961). This is one of the few serious treatments of these themes in recent philosophy.

a sharper distinction between role relations and personal relations than I should want to do; as when he considers a hypothetical case where a teacher of psychology notices abnormal hysterical behaviour in a pupil, and he says that the teacher will have to switch temporarily from a personal relation to one in which he looks on the pupil as an 'object' whose abnormalities he must try to understand with the help of his professional psychological knowledge.[1] But surely the relation of teacher to pupil is also a role relation, with some restraints as well as spontaneity appropriate to it. Personal and role relations are interwoven, and not always clearly separated. We cannot banish the *persona* from the person, even in some of our closest relations, any more than the person from the *persona*. So it is surely important to see how each can survive in the other.

The notion of *persona* answers to the impersonal aspects of morality; it stands for detachment from 'proper names', the attempt to look objectively at a situation, at rights and obligations and at the requirements of the job to be done. We saw the Existentialist case against role morality was that it represented a way in which a person could hide behind his 'functions' and seek security and significance through them.[2] The case, we said, was overdrawn; to take the obligations of a role seriously need not be '*mauvaise foi*'. There are some roles — marital ones, obviously, for instance — into which a person can enter so intimately that he can hardly be said to be using them as means of evading personal decisions (although, of course, he — or more likely the old-fashioned she — *may* use marriage just for this). On the contrary, these roles are likely to call out the most personal of qualities. But there are also roles, particularly those connected with 'public faces' where to identify oneself too closely with the role can lead to sticking out one's chest and taking oneself too seriously. Here, if the 'person' is to preserve himself in the *persona*, he needs

[1] *Op. cit.* p. 29. [2] See above, p. 154.

inner detachment and a sense of humour, humour being, as Bergson saw, the great deflater of men who behave like bits of mechanism [1] (as they would if some accounts of role behaviour are to be believed).

The possibility of detachment may be important theoretically as well as ethically; for, if it can happen, it is evidence against the view which would turn an individual simply into an assemblage of roles. The notion of the 'amateur' sometimes stands for a person who can carry out a role without complete self-identification.[2] Amateurs may be very able indeed; but they can also be dilettantes, if not downright incompetent. An amateur can detach himself from professional status, but if he is to claim 'amateur status' (itself an achieved role), he must be able to do the work or play the game with some expertise. So again, the notions of personal choice and personal style cannot be cut off entirely from role performance and the performance of function. Just as we saw that someone may enter into a role relationship such as marriage in a way which calls out his most intimate personal qualities, so a person may throw his creative powers into a piece of work which, externally regarded, can be seen as a role and function.[3] There are, of course, problems for the creative individual and particularly for the 'amateur' in a highly institutionalized and professionalized society. They will not be met by setting up the purely free individual on the one hand over against rule-bound 'unauthentic' bureaucracy on the other. Also, there are limits to what I, being myself with my powers and

[1] Cf. *Le Rire* (numerous editions), *passim*.

[2] Cf. H. H. Gerth and C. Wright Mills, *Character and Social Structure*, p. 110, where this is suggested, but not developed.

[3] In *Function, Purpose and Powers* I used the notion of 'Vocation' in talking about ways of working from inner springs of action not just describable behaviouristically. I tried there to show how, to adapt a Kantianism, 'vocations without functions are empty, and functions without vocations are blind'. See especially Chapters IX and X.

lack of powers, can choose to be. *Non omnia possumus omnes.* Sartre himself sees this. 'While I must *play at* being a café waiter in order to be one, still it would be in vain for me to play at being a diplomat or a sailor, for I would not be one. This inapprehensible *fact* of my condition, this impalpable difference which distinguishes this drama of realization from drama pure and simple is what causes the for-itself, while choosing the *meaning* of its situation and while constituting itself as the foundation of itself in situation, *not to choose* its position.' [1]   I cannot, like the souls in the Myth of Er in Plato's *Republic*, choose to be born a worker or a bourgeois. Sartre calls this 'facticity'. Genet's play *The Balcony* shows a brothel where the prostitutes humour the clients by letting them dress up and act the roles of their fantasies, one an archbishop, for instance, another a judge. When a revolution breaks out in the city outside, they try to take up these roles in earnest, with absurd results.

Where, then, is the individual in all this? I have said he can enter with personal style into his roles; he can also look at them and himself in them with detachment. There is yet another way in which he is distinguishable from any particular role, or even from an assemblage of roles: through the all too familiar and often painful problem of conflicts between the claims of different roles on time and attention, and even between the obligations to which they point.[2] I doubt whether any society can be so simple that such conflicts never arise, nor so streamlined that there is never any problem in solving them. Certainly this is not so in our own society where role conflict is endemic; here, a person must make his judgment on priorities as best he

[1] *Being and Nothingness*, p. 83.

[2] Recent literature on organizations stresses the compromises which individuals work out amongst the conflicting pressures which go on within the life of big organizations. See, for instance, Melville Dalton, *Men who Manage* (New York, 1959).

can. Plato, indeed, in the *Republic* presents a society as a harmonious system of roles and functions, and looks to justice as the principle of minding one's own business to secure freedom from conflict. But here is a model of a society constructed from outside in imagination: '*We* will impress upon our city . . .' say Socrates, Glaucon and Adeimantus. The political role is to be played by philosopher statesmen, and even here there is supposed to be no conflict of roles, since politics is subordinated to philosophy. But it is here in the end that the harmony breaks down, and it breaks down precisely where Plato, himself a philosopher and a would-be politician, must have known the conflict in his own experience.

Which, then, comes first: the person or the *persona*? This may well be one of those unanswerable 'chicken and egg' questions, unanswerable not only because of the speculative nature of anything that can be said about social origins. There is an interesting study in the aetiology of the two notions in Hubert Mauss' Huxley Memorial Lecture.[1] Mauss says he is not talking about psychological self-consciousness, but about the moral, juridical and metaphysical notion of the 'person'. Evidence he brings from ethnography shows how members of a clan, perhaps with a totemic name, are distinguished by names associated with social positions which others may inherit. This makes the problem of tracing genealogies realistically very difficult: there may be a conflation of generations under the same name. Also a person may have different names in different contexts, in ritual for instance,[2] or at different stages of his life. The name in each case gives him social significance. Mauss then goes on to look at the words *persona* and πρόσωπον in the Roman and Greek sources of our own

[1] 'Une Catégorie de l'esprit humain: la notion de personne celle de "moi"', *Journal of the Royal Anthropological Institute* (1938), vol. 68, p. 263.

[2] Compare the 'name in religion' given to a monk or nun.

culture. In what follows I supplement what he says from another and fuller treatment of these notions to which he refers.[1] *Persona* is originally a mask, through which comes the sound of an actor's voice (*personare*). It then becomes a role in drama (a *dramatis persona*), and thus a social role, often linked with a verb, e.g. *personam gerere*, or *sustinere*. In ancient and mediaeval times different social roles were associated with special dress, perhaps a carry-over from drama and ritual. Nowadays we more or less dress alike, yet when we switch our roles we speak of 'changing our hat'. It must have been difficult for actors in ancient drama to convey nuances of character through their masks. An Elizabethan stage direction 'Here miser leans up against a wall and grows generous', might have needed a change of masks to be effected in ancient drama. A mask can be changed; it cannot suddenly break into a smile. Moreover, the old notion of the *persona* as a mask in a drama has reappeared in another form under the fashionable notion of 'the image'. It is a generally accepted psychological fact that we cannot be directly aware of all the facts and complex features of any person or situation, and this selectivity can be deliberately played upon by those who want to build up an 'image' which sets them in a favourable light. Not only political parties employ public relations men to do just this. Sometimes the concern over the 'image' may be a manifestation of what Erich Fromm[2] calls 'the marketing orientation': people want to put themselves across.[3] But there is also a keeping up of appearances which can be a matter of role morality, as when a doctor will not say things that might embarrass a colleague before his

[1] S. Schlossmann, *Persona und πρόσωπον im Recht und im christlichen Dogma* (Leipzig, 1906).

[2] *Man for Himself* (London, 1949), pp. 67 ff.

[3] Daniel J. Boorstin's book, *The Image* (New York and London, 1961), is a *cri de cœur* on how 'the image' is becoming 'a pseudo-event, displacing realities'.

patient; whatever he may say to him in private, he will try to save his face (note the familiar phrase) in public. This play acting is sometimes justified by role loyalties, or by tact (bedside manners, for instance); it becomes ethically dubious if one is taken in by one's own act or is cynical about it. It shows that the dramatic aspect of a role is too deep-seated to be only a metaphor, or something that can be eliminated.[1]

To return to the fortunes of the notion of *persona* in Roman times. When the word is used to mean a human being, it is not just equally renderable by, e.g., *homo*; it means one who belongs to the category of humankind, and is sometimes used with an adjective distinguishing special status — *persona libera*, *persona vilis*, etc. It is used in this categorizing sense in Roman Law, where cases are distinguished as concerned with *personae*, with *res*, or with *actiones*. In its legal use, it stands particularly for the notion of someone being a subject of rights, including a corporate body. It is thus not just a naturalistic notion of a human being, but rather, an institutional notion. A *persona* has *Conditio* (his family ranking), *Status* (his civil position) and *Munus* (his functions in civil and military life).

The Greek word πρόσωπον also has a close association with drama, although originally (in Homer, for instance) it just meant a face, and then a person having the face. In drama it can be used alternatively with προσωπεῖον for a mask, and then for a dramatic role. With the Stoics in particular it is used for the notion of a human role in the universe, thought

[1] Erving Goffmann, in 'The Presentation of Self in Everyday Life' (University of Edinburgh Social Sciences Research Centre, 1956), and in 'Behaviour in Public Places' (Free Press, Ill., 1964) has collected a range of examples of this sort of thing, showing how widespread stylized behaviour with its tacit understanding and conventions is in social relationships. Through it an individual conveys his definition of the situation to others. 'All the world's a stage' is thus at least a half-truth.

of as carrying with it moral status. In its later legal uses it is probably simply a rendering of *persona*.

The interest in both words lies in the way they are used to refer to people as not just biological individuals.[1] They have strong links with ritual and drama (ancient drama in Greece was after all a form of ritual) and they become terms for the human being as having moral and social significance. So in traditional use there is not an antithesis between a notion of the pure individual 'I', free and solitary but of absolute worth, and on the other hand a notion of the conventional carrier of roles and functions. The notion of the value and status of the individual has developed along with the categories which expressed his social significance. This need not imply that his metaphysical value can be reduced to his social significance; rather it shows that ideas of the former have come through deepening those of the latter. The decisive steps were taken in Stoicism and Christianity, with the emphasis on conscience reinforcing the conception of the human person as a bearer of rights in the moral community.

Mr. Bernard Mayo[2] has defined a personal relation as an instance of knowledge by acquaintance, where the individual so known also has knowledge by acquaintance. (This individual table of which I have knowledge by acquaintance presumably has not such knowledge of me.) He says each personal relation, as a unique happening, is amoral, since he sees morality as dependent on rules citing universalizable properties and classes, which are known by description. He therefore dismisses the notion of respect for persons as a moral notion. While he is surely right in seeing individuals not as just bundles of properties, can there be knowledge of them by acquaintance which is quite

[1] I shall not try to follow the words *persona* and πρόσωπον as they became technical words in Trinitarian doctrine, except to remark that whatever they meant here, they did not mean separate individuals.

[2] *The Logic of Personality* (London, 1952).

free from knowledge of them through their properties? Also respect for persons as a moral notion is not just awareness of individuals; it expresses a conviction about their status.

The romantic notion of the bare subjective 'I' and the behaviouristic notion of the incumbent of a role and function can be split off from this as limiting concepts. But in actual fact can we identify the pure subject in action apart from the social and institutional support represented by the notion of the human person? This is not to say the subject is only the incumbent of roles, though it is of course possible abstractly to consider him just as this. So considered, his significance will lie in his function. This was a starting-point of one strand of Greek ethics, where the significance of, e.g., a doctor lies in his function, ἔργον, as doctor, and his 'virtue' in the role performance of being a good doctor. But the Greek moralists could not just rest there; one wants to be able to talk about the 'good man' and not only the 'good doctor'. So we find an extension of the concept of function into that of the function of being a man *simpliciter*. The good man is then the man who carries out well the function of being a human being. Not only Aristotle, but the Stoics, Epictetus for instance, use such language in looking on morality as playing a role in a world which, if not a drama, is at any rate an 'economy' in which all things have their proper part after their kind. This is behind the notion of the Law of Nature as it has come down particularly from the Stoics. It is a moral and metaphysical notion, setting out the principles things and notably human beings should follow if they are to fulfil their 'natures'. Again we see how the notion of a human being and also of 'nature' are not just descriptive notions; they are value laden, indicating a status in the world. From the point of view of the Law of Nature human beings are not just members of the biological species *homo sapiens*, but seen as having a *social role* in the universe. So 'natural' and 'human' become role

concepts with a normative overtone, calling attention to the
obligation to live according to this social role. We may say
that this is an undue extension of the notions of role and
function. They can be properly used of specific relationships and specific things done; can they be used as blanket
terms covering the innumerable relationships and innumerable things one does in the course of living a human life?
Moreover, from one point of view we might say that all
the ways in which people can live are equally human, and
count nothing human alien to us. But from another point
of view the old notion of the Law of Nature may bring out
something important for morality. It may be a way of
saying that morality need not only be a matter either of
following the *mores* or of freely choosing how to live and
seeing social morality as *mauvaise foi*. It can also be a
matter of *discovering* how it is possible for people to live
together in ways which lead to an increasing capacity for
mutual trust and moral growth. It may be misleading to
say there is a code of universal principles; but, as we saw in
Chapter V, there may be a procedural interpretation of the
notion of Natural Justice which would set a limit to complete normative relativism — if, that is to say, we are prepared to look on morality as a rational matter at all.

'Natural Law' has also included the idea of the human
person as such as a status over and above the special kinds
of status belonging to some people and not to others. If
we look on the notions of rights and obligations as arising
out of the kinds of relations, ascriptive or contractual, in
which we stand to people, it is obviously tempting to bring
into line the notion of obligations to any other human being
as such by talking, as the Stoics did, of the actions proper
to a human being. If we do not use the notion of a general
human role and function, we can rephrase the question by
asking whether, besides particular obligations in particular
roles, ethical systems include ideas of what would be right
or wrong when done to anyone, whosoever he was. One

might imagine an extension of moral relations thus happening logically through the character of moral judgment itself,
by which reasons are demanded to justify differential treatment; and in time, in some cases, the reasons getting
threadbare. Or we can look empirically at ethical systems
of which we have information and see whether there are some
actions which are looked on as crimes whoever does them
and to whomever they are done: murder, for instance, as
deliberate killing of another for private purposes, as distinct
from institutionalized killing for public purposes, such as
killing enemies in war, executing criminals or attacking
feuding clansmen. The fact that there may be institutionalized exceptions to a general prohibition shows how difficult
it is to draw a line between things which may be considered
right or wrong if done to anyone, not just to a special class
of people, and things which are considered right and wrong
in a particular role. Nevertheless, I think it is possible
broadly to distinguish moral notions of general as well as of
special application. How far this is a distinction drawn
somehow in most societies is something on which anthropologists can supply evidence. (In any case, we need not be
wedded to arguments *e consensu gentium*.) This distinction
is certainly drawn in the 'universal' religions; in fact
this is almost the definition of a universal religion. These
also condemn what is called in the New Testament
προσωπολημψία,[1] 'respect of persons' in the sense of looking
snobbishly at the special status and not through it at the
human being. I find impressive Bergson's contention that
an attitude of outgoing concern for human kind found in
these religions is not just a logical extension of narrower
circles of obligation, but makes a forward leap of faith and
love.[2] Yet aspirations of faith and love towards humanity,

---

[1] Romans ii, 11; Colossians iii, 25; Epistle of St. James ii, 1.

[2] Cf. his *Les Deux Sources de la morale et de la religion* (numerous
editions). I should want to qualify, however, his somewhat romantic account of 'mysticism'. (See my *Function, Purpose and Powers*, pp. 143 ff.)

like the work of individual reformers, are hardly socially
effective unless they can find appropriate institutional em-
bodiments.   Charters of human rights in international law
come somewhere between the two.   They give formal
juridical expression to universalist moral aspirations, but the
institutions for upholding them have only very partial
governmental powers.

The institutional side is therefore too deep-seated in actual
life to be by-passed by a purely personal morality.   Yet very
little special attention has been given by philosophical
moralists to these institutional aspects.   Perhaps the one
classical essay is Bradley's 'My Station and its Duties',[1] an
essay as exasperating as it is trenchant.   'If you could be
as good as your world,' says Bradley, 'you would be better
than most likely you are' ('world' here being 'the morality
already existing to hand in laws, institutions, moral opinions
and feelings'), and 'to wish to be better than the world is
to be already on the threshold of immorality'.   On the
threshold, but not necessarily over it.   Bradley sees that to
confine myself within 'my station and its duties' is in-
adequate in any actual community we know, though he
hints that it might be adequate in an ideal community.   The
whole essay is a polemic against the individualist who thinks
he has no duties except those he has freely thought out and
assumed for himself.   But he dismisses cavalierly the individual behind the rights and duties: like Bosanquet and
other idealist philosophers writing about society, he ap-
preciates how society exists through a network of institutions, but has little appreciation for the conflicts and stresses
this produces for its members.

To-day, even more than when Bradley wrote, life seems
more and more to be lived in the setting of large-scale as
well as small-scale institutions, and this can be felt acutely
as a problem by those for whom the final moral values are
personal.   Yet a morality simply of direct 'I-Thou' relations

[1] *Ethical Studies* (2nd edition, Oxford, 1927), pp. 199 ff.

cannot take account of the host of indirect relations in which
we stand to people, nor the impersonal element which arises
even in personal morality, and *a fortiori* in the morality of
official institutional relations.   A *purely* personalist morality,
since it cannot come to terms with these, must either abandon
them to anarchy (which is unrealistic) or to external regula-
tion (which may be all too realistic).

On the other hand if we press the 'mask' metaphor and
take so mechanical and literal a notion of the *persona* that it
becomes just something through which the right sort of
noises sound (*personant*), we shall never catch the conversa-
tion-like nuances by which role performances are also found
to be relationships between people.

CHAPTER NINE

LIVING WITH
ORGANIZATION MAN [1]

We started from the not very controversial observation that ethics and sociology are both concerned with social relations in social situations, and went on to say that sociologists do well to look at ways in which moral values can be involved both theoretically in the definition of a 'social situation' and practically in the methods chosen to study it. We have also said that moral judgments are made in *social* situations. That moralists would do well to look at sociological studies of these has been stated in general rather than by particular illustration. It needs substantiating by examples rather than precept; I shall now try to do this by calling attention to some recent sociological work in the study of organizations. There are some obvious reasons for this choice.

1. Large organizations are probably the most characteristic feature of contemporary society, at any rate western society, and they increasingly impinge on the ways we live our lives. These organizations are both public and private: government departments, business corporations, professional organizations, educational organizations, recreational organizations and so on and so on. That life is increasingly lived in and with the help of these is, I believe, a much more important feature of contemporary society than are controversies between socialist collectivism and individual enterprise. Large organizations can only be wished away if we can be content with a much more rudimentary standard of

[1] The title might lead some readers to expect a description of what it is like to be the mistress of the General Manager. I hasten to assure them there is no such *double entendre*.

goods and services than we have come to take for granted, and if fewer people are to have claims on these. Those of us who live and work in universities are having to adjust ourselves to the change from the ways of a fairly informal and not very large community to those of a big organization; and those whose hearts, like the author's, are in the horse and buggy era of the university rather than the era of Organization Man, do not find the change in our ways easy. Nor do we want to make it uncritically.

2. The study of organizations is concerned with social units whose boundaries it is relatively possible to draw, though what goes on within them is of course also affected by what is happening in the wider social environment. Thus they form reasonably recognizable units, partly planned and self-contained, but also *milieux* for unplanned and competing relations. They can therefore provide manageable units of study which are streamlined versions of some of the problems, including moral problems, of interlocking human relations in society in the wider sense.

3. Large organizations are networks of relationships between people acting and reacting on each other, sometimes in accordance with intended ways of furthering the purpose of the organization; sometimes in ways which are intended, though not in terms of the official purpose; and sometimes in ways not intended by anyone. These by-activities may either help to fortify the official purpose or to frustrate it. In either case decisions, both administrative and policy decisions, including the moral judgments which can come into these, can be made more intelligently if there is some realistic awareness of this complexity. A corollary of this is that even official policy is subject to considerations other than those deducible from the formal relationships within the organization, and account has to be taken of this in trying to set up criteria of its 'rationality'.

4. The theory of organizations includes questions of 'operational research'. This is concerned with trying to

bridge the gulf between unanalysed abstractions, such as 'efficiency', or 'public service', or 'modernization', and actual decisions. It can thus provide a context for studying how such abstractions can function if one wants neither to be Utopian about them (i.e. idealistically indifferent about the hard facts of practice) nor to be cynical (i.e. using them emotively for persuasive purposes, while regarding them as vacuous). Such operational research may provide object lessons in thinking about the functions of similar abstractions in ethical and political thinking.

5. Sophisticated contemporary studies of organizations recognize conflict and tensions as facts of life. This is partly because participants in organizations have multiple roles and role sets, unofficial as well as official, within the organization, and roles such as political ones which have ramifications outside it. This can raise questions of an ethical kind, concerning, for instance, the degree of loyalty due to the organization and how to reconcile this with other claims. The organization cannot therefore be seen as a harmonious self-contained unit, in which problems can even in principle always be solved according to the rules. The 'solution' of one problem may bring others in its train; and wisdom may lie in being able to decide which problem to live with at any given time.

This means that the classical description of 'rational bureaucracy' as given by Max Weber is seen to be too simple, though indeed Weber must be acknowledged as the pioneer in seeing the growing importance of 'bureaucratic' types of organization and authority in modern society. I shall follow the excellent summary of his definitions given by Tom Burns and G. M. Stalker.[1]

---

[1] *The Management of Innovation* (Tavistock Publications, 1961), pp. 105–106. Cf. also M. Weber, *The Theory of Social and Economic Organization* (tr. Henderson and Parsons). W. Hodge, 1947, pp. 329–334 (Free Press, Glencoe, Ill., 1947).

(1) The organization operates according to a body of laws or rules, which are consistent and have normally been intentionally established.

(2) Every official is subject to an impersonal order by which he guides his actions. In turn his instructions have authority only in so far as they conform with this generally understood body of rules; obedience is due to his office, not to him as an individual.

(3) Each incumbent of an office has a specified sphere of competence, with obligations, authority, and powers to compel obedience strictly defined.

(4) The organization of offices follows the principle of hierarchy; that is, each lower office is under the control and supervision of a higher one.

(5) The supreme head of the organization, and only he, occupies his position by appropriation, by election, or by being designated as successor. Other offices are filled, in principle, by free selection, and candidates are selected on the basis of 'technical' qualifications. They are appointed, not elected.

(6) The system also serves as a career ladder. There is promotion according to seniority or achievement. Promotion is dependent on the judgement of superiors.

(7) The official who, in principle, is excluded from any ownership rights in the concern, or in his position, is subject to discipline and control in the conduct of his office.

This can now be seen to work on too simple a model of bureaucracy, as well as of 'rationality'. It shows rationality for the person in a subordinate role as simply acting according to the book of rules; for the top people rationality is not defined by Weber. Here the model has been that of classical economic man, where rationality consists in always doing what would maximize interests, in this case those of the organization. This assumes there is an optimum solution, which administrative man seeks if he is rational; it is an essentially Benthamite notion, which has reappeared in modern dress in Games Theory where rationality consists in 'minimaxing', seeking to maximize advantage and minimize risks of loss by choosing the optimum utility among the alternatives. The assumption here is that the alternatives are calculable, and their consequences can be forecast. Such a model of rational optimum decision can have its uses in situations where there are a finite number of variables; where alternatives are known and limited, and where there can be a preference ranking among them.

In contrast, administrative decisions and policy decisions for organizations are likely to have to make do with what H. A. Simon calls 'bounded rationality'.[1] This works on a more complex theory of knowledge, where the 'situation' as perceived is recognized to be only a simplification of the actual facts of the real world. The 'situation' does not come ready packaged; it is interpreted in terms of 'relevant' or 'strategic' factors; but what is not realized or is ignored may take revenge for its omission in the unforeseen consequences of a decision. For 'the capacity of the human mind for formulating and solving complex problems is very small compared with the size of the problems whose solution is required for objectively rational behaviour in the real world'.[2] The range of the human mind can be extended by collaborative collection of information, 'data processing' by computer, and so on, but the essential point of selectivity remains. Also, collaboration for extending powers of thought and action beyond those of the individual produces its problems as well as its advantages. 'It is only because individual human beings are limited in knowledge, foresight, skill and

[1] Cf. H. A. Simon, *Models of Man* (New York, 1957), pt. iv, pp. 196 ff., 'Administrative Rationality and Decision Making'; also his *Administrative Behaviour*, and Simon and March, *Organizations* (New York, 1958), pp. 137 ff.   [2] *Models of Man*, p. 198.

time that organizations are useful instruments for the achievement of human purpose; and it is only because organized groups of human beings are limited in ability to agree on goals, to communicate, and to cooperate that organizing becomes for them a "problem".'[1] This does not mean that decisions made in such a context cannot be 'rational'; it means that rationality will involve taking account of its own 'boundedness'. It will involve looking for viable solutions rather than ideal solutions (in Simon's terminology 'satisficing' rather than 'optimicing'), and seeing that there may be critical times at which an imperfect decision is better than none.

Rational behaviour is not of course the same as ethical behaviour; it may be concerned with questions of policy, interest, advantage, which are not directly ethical (though in a context of complex human relations these may well have ethical implications and there may indeed be a moral obligation to take account of them). On the views that I have argued earlier, ethical behaviour, while not exhaustive of rational behaviour, need not be irrational behaviour. Indeed, the rationality characteristic of at any rate the more difficult and interesting moral judgments may well be 'bounded rationality' in situations of uncertainty, where neither action by rule nor clear perception of consequences has a self-evident last word.

'Bounded rationality', whether in moral decisions or decisions on questions of, e.g., efficiency, is not only due to ignorance of fact. It is also due to the ways in which people see the facts of a situation as coloured by their own role in regard to it. This may be particularly the case in interpreting situations in organizations and institutions, where how a person sees a situation may not only depend on his own social and intellectual background, but on his role in the organization, or on which of his multiple roles he puts first. Tom Burns has a good illustration of this in a paper

[1] *Ibid.* p. 199.

'The Directions of Activity and Communication in a Departmental Executive Group'.[1] This is a study of how four executives in an engineering firm reported that they spent their time when away from their desks. There was general agreement that they spent their time talking to people;[2] but when the accounts of what each executive said he talked about to the other executives were compared, they revealed significant discrepancies. There was fair agreement over how much time was spent in talking about 'Research and Developments'; but not so over 'Production Matters' and 'Personnel'. Burns' conclusion is not that the executives were inaccurate in their reports, still less that they were lying, but that they distorted the content of what they thought they were talking about in terms of what they were interested in through their special roles.

The moral is that one cannot be sure that different participants in a situation are concerning themselves with the same 'image' of the situation; there is a problem of communication here if attempts at co-operation or agreed decisions are not to be at cross purposes. Moreover, the participants in an organization do not simply play their complementary roles within the organization. They are also human beings, adaptive and non-adaptive, anxious, ambitious, loyal, suspicious, generous. So there will be conflicts of interests and loyalties not only between different groups within the organization, but in the minds of each of its members from the top to the bottom.

To realize this makes for an approach to problems, both moral and practical, more complex than is allowed for in taking account of simple alternatives of efficiency and inefficiency, loyalty and disloyalty, rate for the job and exploitation. Indeed, what is thought to constitute any of these will depend on a context of moral assumptions, which will

[1] *Human Relations* (1954), vol. VII, pp. 73–97.
[2] i.e. talking to people as part of the job; what they talked about as coffee gossip was not counted.

vary at different times and cannot just be taken as constant.
The notion of the 'rate for the job', for instance, if it is not
just left to the mechanisms of the market, will be discussed
and bargained for with assumptions about acceptable
standards of living in the wider community.   There are
other still more 'value laden' issues; for instance, terms
on which people will collaborate with the goals of the
organization and the degree of commitment that can
properly be expected of them.   This is a region where
personal value judgments are bound to enter in, for though
'terms on which people will collaborate' could seem to be
something just to be ascertained as a question of fact, it
connects with the degree of commitment which can 'properly' be expected, and implies a decision on what ought or
ought not to be asked.   A statement to the effect that every
organization will exact as much commitment as it can could
not only be questioned as a matter of fact, but also it might
be said that on ethical grounds members should try to
prevent it from extracting a total commitment.

    That there is indeed an argument here not only about the
facts of organizations, but also about their ethics, has been
abundantly shown by W. H. Whyte's onslaught on one
view of the ethos of 'Organization Man'.[1]   The burden
of his attack is that those concerned with personal relations
and loyalties within organizations, along with their sociological advisers, assume a culture based on the ethos of
the organization as an essentially harmonious and indeed
beneficent unity, where the needs of the individual are met
by adapting to the needs of the group, and where tensions
can be removed by better scientific understanding and social
engineering.   Whyte attacks these comfortable assumptions not only because he thinks people ought sometimes to
take a stand and fight the organization, but also because he
cares that they should have personal lives, political lives,
intellectual lives, which are not only lived in its terms.

    [1] *The Organization Man* (New York and London, 1957).

His predilections are forcibly shared by one of his reviewers, Professor George Homans.[1]

'On top of all this, the organization takes such good care of its men that they may come to look on its ways not as habits to be put up with if they want to keep out of trouble but as virtues to be loved for themselves alone. In America, we were ready to love them anyway. Americans were never quite the rugged individualists they professed themselves to be. Rather, their easy associativeness was both their glory and their danger. When all three forces — American culture, corporate bureaucracy, and social science — work in line, the pressure may squash out qualities that give the life to men and nations. *The Organization Man* ends with an old plea in a new form, a plea that we render to the organization only what is the organization's — our service, not our souls.

With this I heartily agree. The individualist is a pretty tough man. In the loosely knit societies of the past, there were plenty of places where he could hole up and glare out at us. And we could trust him to do it. Today the holes are getting fewer. We may need to take some thought how to make the world safe for him, for the world's sake as well as his own.'

There is little doubt that this candid avowal has stirred up a lively discussion of ethical assumptions that were slipping into the study of organizations. These assumptions encouraged the belief that techniques could be related to 'a finite achievable harmony'; that conflicts are due to misunderstandings and breakdowns in communication which should be capable of being eliminated by applying the methods of science to human relations; and that the needs of the individual could be met in terms of the needs of the

[1] 'Bureaucracy as Big Brother', *The Listener*, Nov. 7, 1957; reprinted in *Sentiments and Activities* (Free Press, Ill., 1962), pp. 125–126. Quoted with permission.

organization. On the question of the facts as distinct from the ethics of conformity, Whyte has been taken up by Melville Dalton in *Men who Manage*, a sociological study largely devoted to showing how scepticism and manipulation can go on under a public image of conformity. He suggests that those who mistake surface conformity in organizations for total conformity and the death of originality should study the ingenuity and evasion that actually goes on, and 'the ethics of protective coloration among thinking animals'.[1] Whyte himself is not in fact altogether innocent of this awareness; what he is after is to question some of the assumptions of a social ethos which he sees creeping into official literature and especially that of training schemes. He would no doubt welcome Dalton's well-documented argument that 'perpetual harmony is alien to all life', that, though areas of conflict may shift, it is unlikely that they can be eliminated entirely.

Another study, which shows how some problems in an organization can be met at the cost of producing others, is that of Alvin W. Gouldner,[2] describing a kind of situation in which there is no ideal solution. Where this is so the cost of a policy has to be measured against its success, 'cost' here not meaning monetary cost (people have always known about this), but the respects in which one problem within an organization is relieved by measures which will exacerbate others. Gouldner showed this in his study of a gypsum plant called 'Oscar Centre', Lakeport, near the Great Lakes in Wisconsin, where a popular lenient management had been replaced by a stricter and more efficient one. The old regime was mixed up with kinship links outside

---

[1] *Men who Manage* (New York, 1959), p. 272. Melville Dalton calls the capacity to cope with this complexity a capacity to 'live with ambiguity'. It gave me pleasure to find his book catalogued in a great University Library in the section 'Useful Arts'.

[2] See especially his *Patterns of Industrial Democracy* and *Wildcat Strike* (London, 1955).

the factory, and other established community relations. There was indulgence, for instance, towards workers taking materials home from the factory for their own purposes. A new manager came with instructions to tighten things up; he tried to be impartial and act through official channels and not through the informal ties (such as the old lieutenants). This produced its tensions, culminating in a 'wildcat strike', which Gouldner judged to be only ostensibly about wage demands, on which grievances, due to the contravention of established expectations based on the older more informal code, had got displaced. (He suggests also that a strike on wages could be made to appear more acceptable to the wives.) The method of trying to resolve this conflict was to make the rules clearer. But insistence on rules encouraged a 'work to rule' mentality (called by Gouldner 'bureaucratic sabotage'). So there was need for closer supervision, and this in turn reinforced the emphasis on rules. Hence a vicious circle with mutual reinforcement, viz.

1
Technological changes, and changes in succession
↓
2
Closer supervision by management
↓
3
Violation of workers' indulgency expectations
↓
4
More aggressive attitude, leading to still closer supervision.

After the strike, an agreement was reached providing procedures for settling grievances at the cost of more bureaucratic rules. This relieved tensions due to informal actions, and enabled disputes to be passed up for higher consideration, but it increased supervision still further. Thus the settlement of the strike included a more centralized bureaucratic direction and definition of rights and obligations, which reduced some tensions, but meant there was less chance of informal communication between workers and supervisors, so that supervisors became even less aware of workers' 'indulgency expectations'.[1] The top management and union officials thus reached a solution in accordance with the interests of their own status and authority, but at the expense of curtailing the initiative of those below them on either side.

. One way of meeting this, in so far as it is due to lack of 'participation' in decisions, is to develop an 'organic' system instead of the mechanistic form. The terms 'mechanistic' and 'organic' are taken from *The Management of Innovation* by Tom Burns and G. M. Stalker. The mechanistic form approximates most closely to the Weberian rules of rational bureaucracy; it is said to be appropriate in stable conditions. The most significant element for our purpose in the summary of its characteristics is that it is a hierarchic system of control, authority and communication, which is reinforced 'by the location of knowledge of actualities exclusively at the top of the hierarchy, while the final reconciliation of distinct tasks and assessment of relevance is made'.[2] In contrast, in the 'organic' form (which is said to be appropriate to changing conditions), there is 'adjustment and continual re-definition of individual tasks through interaction with others', and 'a lateral rather than a vertical direction of communication through the organization, communication between people of different rank, also, resembling consultation rather than demand'. The extent of the individual's commitment and responsibility is also less clearly delimited.[3]

[1] Gouldner has shown that, not only in conflict situations, *succession* tends to weaken informal structures, and so at any rate temporarily to strengthen bureaucratic organization. (Cf. 'Succession and Bureaucracy' in *Studies in Leadership* (New York, 1950), pp. 644–659.

[2] *Op. cit.* p. 120.   [3] *Ibid.* p. 121.

A first reaction to the summary of the 'organic' form is that, just as Weber's rational bureaucracy is too simple to be true, this is too good to be true. When looked into more closely, it will be seen that it too produces its problems and its human cost. The authors are well aware of this, unlike Mary Parker Follett, who was a pioneer in this way of thinking about management.[1] She saw that while classical economic theory made participation in group activity instrumental to other satisfactions (e.g. being paid money), there were also satisfactions (and otherwise) in the actual process of the group activity itself. She could be starry-eyed as well as sophisticated about this, on paper at least, though not, I believe, in actual negotiations. One question is whether the continual need for discussion and communication will mean that people become more interested in the procedures by which decisions are reached and in having a share in reaching them than in getting on with the actual job for which the organization exists. While these procedures may lead to a more widespread sense of participation, no one can say that they are not time-consuming. They also depend on a widely shared intuitive morality and shared attitude, beyond the specific obligations of role and function. Therefore, alike in moral effort, time, and thought, the commitment of members to the organization is much more diffuse and unlimited than the 'nine to five' commitment to a limited role with limited responsibilities under a hierarchic system of authority. This again may be as it should be; but the cost must be reckoned (the loss to other roles, such as those of private life; the possibility of 'possessing one's soul' apart from the organization; and the preoccupation with methods and procedures). It is also useless to think that such more 'democratic' procedures in fact relieve those at the top of responsibility and lighten their

---

[1] Cf. especially *Dynamic Administration: The Collected Papers of Mary Parker Follett*, edited by M. C. Metcalfe and L. Urwick (Management Publications Trust, London, 1941).

load. It is arguable that the 'boss' in a hierarchic organization, whose decisions have to be accepted, has a less exacting time than the head of an 'organic' body who needs to consult and allow discussion at every level. Indeed one of the major problems in modern organizations (not just firms, but, e.g., government departments and increasingly universities as they are now developing) is the demand they make on the people at the top. Contrary to popular belief, these get greater and not less with attempts to make the organization more 'democratic'.

An instance of this is the effect of the combination of the official organization with its official purpose and the organization as a field within which people seek to pursue careers.[1] In the older kind of mechanistic hierarchical organization, promotion could be decided by superiors by considerations of seniority or technical competence in a clearly defined sphere. It is tempting to look for a formula, and so produce an impersonal (and obviously universalizable) basis for decision. But fairness in the sense of equity does not consist in operating with one formula alone. In the 'organic' kind of organization a larger and less specific range of competence and capacity for a more difficult kind of shared authority becomes relevant. This again may be as it should be; but judgments will be more difficult to make, and there will be bound to be people with claims of an obviously definable sort, such as seniority, who will complain that they are being passed over in favour of people whose claims are less definable. In order that justice may be seen to be done, there may be suggestions for relieving the tension between an organization as a community with a common purpose and an organization as a field within which people hope to have a career, by asking for more formalized procedures for review and promotion. Here

[1] Burns and Stalker (*The Management of Innovation*, pt. II, Chapter VII) have drawn attention to this double aspect of life in organizations.

again, there will be a need to be able to look with a critical eye at unintended consequences of *prima facie* plausible proposals. For instance, to take an example from the modern university world, the suggestion has been put forward that all university teachers below the rank of professor should have their status and claims to promotion reviewed every year. Apart from the question of how much this is going to add to the pressures on the time of the people at the top, it again raises questions of whether disadvantages might outweigh advantages. They may not; what is being said here is that they should be diagnosed and taken into consideration with open eyes. For if the object of the exercise is to cause the board concerned with promotions to have to take account at regular intervals of evidence other than that brought forward on the initiative of the head of a department, it is difficult to see how this could be collected apart from some means of monitoring which would surely take away from the wide freedom at present enjoyed by university teachers to do their own work in their own way with the minimum of supervision. Again, people may be prepared to stomach this change; but if so, they must know the implications of what they are asking for. It is also at least arguable that to know one is constantly under judgment may add to status anxiety rather than relieve it; it does not mean that there will not be an area of conflict, but that it will be shifted. Some cases of injustice would no doubt be met; but at the expense of heightening the emphasis on the organization as a field for careers, along with the amount of time and thought given to this aspect of it. Time and thought are scarce resources; the point is that choices of how to use them have to be made.

This is an instance of the cost of choices in unwanted consequences as well as wanted ones. The capacity to diagnose unintended consequences and so to make us more aware of the cost of the choices before us need not be an exclusive skill of sociologists. It might be said to be a matter merely of exercising a bit of realistic imagination. But, for all that, it is not a common skill; perhaps because of the fact already noted in considering 'bounded rationality', that a situation as diagnosed is in any case only a simplified version of the total situation, and, besides this, that the factors people take into account in reading the situation may be affected by how they see their roles in relation to it. A sociologist may manage to divest himself more easily of some of these reasons for selective interpretation, even if he can never reach the total view of omniscience or be the complete 'impartial spectator'. Moreover, he has trained himself to think in terms of reactions of multiple relationships on one another rather than of single strands of cause and effect. He has meditated on the simple but often neglected truth that a relation of A to B is also a relation of B to A; and probably also involves relations to C, D, E . . . and their relations back to each other and to A and B as well.

The problem of unintended consequences, and especially unintended consequences of what may seem eminently desirable aims, is the theme of Philip Selznick's *T.V.A. and the Grass Roots*.[1] This was a study made in the mid-1940's of the Tennessee Valley Authority, a public corporation set up by Congress in 1933 for the operation of electricity, fertilizer plants, irrigation, and flood control in the development of a depressed region. It was set up with a 'grass roots' policy of working with and through local associations, both statutory and voluntary. Such a policy of local 'democratic participation' meant that the Authority was caught up in the tensions of bodies on the spot; it had difficulty (but succeeded) in resisting colour discrimination in appointments. Moreover, it was found that the practical needs of the organization drove it towards alliances with certain well-organized local interests, above all the agriculturalists. Interpreting unanalysed abstractions such as

[1] *T.V.A. and the Grass Roots: A Study in the Sociology of Formal Organization* (University of California Press, 1949).

'institutions near to the people' in context meant that the Authority had to adapt itself not so much to the people in general as to the actually existing institutions which had the power to smooth or block its way, with all the problems for a liberal outlook which this involved. Alvin Gouldner takes Selznick to task over this study for fastening on the organizational and structural tendencies which militate against democratic practices, instead of those that support and encourage them.[1] This is hard; it is clear that Selznick's own sympathies are with the ideals of the T.V.A., and that he gives the emphasis he does because he thinks believers in such ideals are more likely to be unrealistically optimist than pessimist. (This applies also to Dr. Reinhold Niebuhr, who is often unjustly charged with cynicism and pessimism in his political writings for the same reason.[2]) 'For the things which are important in the analysis of democracy are those which bind the hands of good men.'[3] Failure to appraise the problems of implementing unanalysed abstractions may well lead to a swing from idealism to cynicism and from Utopianism to disillusion. Selznick has diagnosed some of the problems in the T.V.A. context without falling for either of these. 'Where such analysis is considered destructive, it is usually because doctrine, assuming an ideological role, is not meant to be analysed. In extreme cases, unanalysed doctrine ceases to operate in action at all, and the real criteria of decision are hidden in a shadowland of unrecognized discretion, determined opportunistically by immediate exigency.'[4]

[1] A. W. Gouldner, 'Metaphysical Pathos and the Theory of Bureaucracy', *American Political Science Quarterly* (1955), vol. 49, pp. 496–507.

[2] Dr. Niebuhr's books, based on his understanding of Christian morality, have been a sustained polemic against Utopianism, and especially self-righteous Utopianism. See, e.g., *An Interpretation of Christian Ethics* (New York and London, 1935).

[3] *T.V.A. and the Grass Roots*, p. 266.

[4] *Ibid.* p. 69. (See also his remarks on Utopianism and opportunism in *Leadership and Administration*, pp. 143 ff.)

o

In discussing moral judgment in Chapter IV, I tried to put forward a view that this was neither simply deduction from principles nor simply calculation of consequences, and that it operates with what we may now call 'bounded rationality' in situations where there may be no simple answer, and where perhaps the only final betrayal may be to refuse to try to come to a decision. Abstractions expressing general aims, such as 'self-realization', 'love of God and one's neighbour', 'the greatest happiness of the greatest number', we saw were not the kind of objective which could be made operational in a straightforward way through clear-cut means to a specific end. They supply, rather, a general orientation for a policy for living, which can be partially, though never entirely, specified through moral principles. The analogy with the working of abstractions such as 'democratic participation' is apparent, though the operational meaning of the ultimate ethical abstractions can be even more elusive. Yet they can supply an orientation which prevents moral judgment from being just *ad hoc* and there are some kinds of behaviour they would exclude on any count. In so far as there is an intention to make moral judgment rational, we saw that it could also be guided by the general requirement to avoid special pleading in our own favour. I suggest that, even more evidently than in personal ethics, this is the sort of view of moral judgments which best fits the complexities of moral situations in institutional and organizational life. Far from calling for a simple morality of rule and rote, the pressures of different claims and interests call for moral intelligence of a high order; where this seems too difficult, demanding also too much moral toughness, we may find instead an amoral ingenuity (the favourite word in the literature is 'manipulation', with its suggestion of fixing things). I have already noted how Chester Barnard, whose books are a mine of wisdom on these questions, speaks of the need for *intelligence* as well as a high sense of responsibility, especially in the moral judgments which high executives have to make. Without the former, the complex morality needed may lead to personal breakdown; without the latter, there may be 'the hopeless confusion of inconsistent expediencies so often described as "incompetence"'.[1] In spite of a popular theological view, here surely is a sphere of moral decisions in which 'love' is not enough, even if it be enough (as I doubt) in the sphere of purely personal relations.

One feature of this complexity is that, in the morality of institutional action, the relations between the personal and impersonal kinds of responsibility come to a head. We have seen that perhaps by definition, but also by direction of interest, personalist discussions of morality in face-to-face relations have had little to say about this. We have also seen that the ethics of role (of which the ethics of institutional actions are an obvious instance) have to take account of previously structured commitments and expectations within a network of relationships. In the case of a role within a formally organized institution, these commitments and expectations may also be structured by the fact that a person has limited powers and limited discretion. Thus there is likely to be a lack of clear coincidence between 'powers', actual power, and responsibility. We have often been told that there should be no power without responsibility; but a problem in modern large-scale institutions (including government) is the need for people to be prepared to take responsibility without commensurate power. In discussing the notion of responsibility I noted the distinction between responsibility as 'answerability', which can be a matter depending on constitutional conventions, and responsibility as ascribing personal power of choice to do or to forbear. In any formal institution there must be some people who, in virtue of their office, are responsible in the sense of answerable for decisions, policies and their

[1] *The Functions of the Executive*, p. 276. (Cf. above, pp. 165-166.)

outcome. This need not mean that they had a major share in making the decision (they may even have had their own reservations about it, or not have been able to prevent what happened). They have, however, to be prepared to take public responsibility without disclosing their private reservations or giving away confidential matter on how the decision was taken (for some things must be discussed confidentially), and particularly they must be prepared to 'carry the can' if things go wrong. This is a feature of the nature of constitutional responsibility in institutional life which can be understood, so that even if it sometimes seems hard in the individual instance, it is possible to accept it impersonally and without resentment. The relevant quality of mind is what the Stoics called *apatheia*, misunderstood in common English parlance as 'apathy' or insensitivity. Rather, it is the capacity to be detached from being influenced by how things touch one's own personal interest and self-esteem, and not to be emotionally involved through these. It is indeed part of the morality of practical reason.

Nevertheless, the lack of coincidence between responsibility and real power to get things done or altered is a genuine problem in institutional morality. Small men may fasten on this as a reason for disclaiming responsibility in the personal sense of power to do or to forbear; larger men may know the discrepancy is there, but not try to shelter behind it. Whereas smaller men may be sticklers for rules, larger men will know no organization can work without discretion.[1] They will not just accept a dissolution of responsibility into formal conventions, and be prepared to go

---

[1] 'Discretion' can cover turning a blind eye to a certain amount of 'institutionalized deviancy' in any organization. The *reductio ad absurdum* of the lack of this is shown when an organization can be made to grind to a halt through 'work to rule'. This can be done by insisting that rules which are in the book as exceptional safeguards be treated as if they were normal practices.

on trying to take personal as well as conventional responsibility through accepting the loneliness of leadership. Our constitutional and institutional arrangements in a liberal democracy are designed to prevent the concentration of responsibility in a single supreme personal leader combining final power as well as formal responsibility. Critics of liberal democracy have pointed to the evasions of responsibility its conventions may make possible; those of us who distrust the *Führer-Prinzip* (we have seen what it can mean), will look on these evasions as a risk to be taken for the sake of a system in which powers and responsibilities can be spread. Yet the temptation to pass the buck is a real one; this is yet another instance of how there is a catch in everything, so that no institutional arrangements will produce Utopia. It is a temptation, particularly because of the very limited actual power of most participants in an organized institution. Yet in an 'organic' system they may all be claiming what Bagehot said were the privileges of monarchy: the right to be informed, the right to encourage, the right to warn. This may be as it should be; but in the end some people must take more responsibility (in both senses of the word) than this. Nevertheless the limits of their practical choice may be curtailed by the 'logic of the situation' in which they have to act, as well as by what others are prepared to accept. Sociological awareness of the logic of situations can help us to appreciate this; it need not, as we have seen, lead to a deterministic view that any given decision *had* to be so and not otherwise. But it can discourage 'scapegoating' and 'conspiratorial' interpretations of situations which turn out badly. This is the more important because to seek explanations of our misfortunes in the machinations of ill-disposed persons is the most primitive and natural way in which we all think until we have become sufficiently sophisticated to think otherwise. Personal causes are easier to understand, and we can also then do something about the misfortune by taking it out on

o 2

the scapegoats. It may well be that the acceptance of re-sponsibility for something which was not in any literal sense 'his fault' by a minister as head of a department, or by others in representative positions, is a civilized relic of this demand for a scapegoat. It is also probably a necessary constitutional convention, and can be taken as such in an impersonal way without resentment.

It can probably be taken in this way the more readily where loyalty to the institution is a strong motive. For, *pace* W. H. Whyte, there *is* a problem of loyalty, which remains when we have had our laugh at Bureaucracy as Big Brother. While we may hold that no institution or organiza-tion should exact a *total* commitment (the Roman Catholic Church, with all its claims, recognizes conscience, and it is possible to leave it), clearly also few organizations would work unless some people were prepared to put more into them than could be stated in a bare contract. By 'total commitment' I am meaning abrogation of judgment and conscience in putting the demands of the organization before all other considerations in all contexts. At the end of that road can stand Eichmann, who went to his death protesting that he was being punished for obedience, and that obedience is praised as a virtue. Loyalty and deep involvement in the purposes of an organization need not mean this abrogation. 'Your representative owes you not his industry only but his judgment', as Burke remarked in another connection.[1] Burke also remarks 'his mature judgment, his enlightened conscience, he ought not to sacrifice to you, to any man, or to any set of men living'. Indeed organizations worth their salt are better served where this is recognized. We should distinguish, of course, between kinds of organizations.[2]

---

[1] *Speech to the Electors of Bristol,* 1774.
[2] An analytic basis for the classification of different kinds of organization by their predominant means of compliance has been given by A. Etzioni, *A Comparative Analysis of Complex Organiza-tions* (Free Press, Ill., 1961). He distinguishes those in which the

Prisons can hardly expect to produce dedicated old lags, while a little subversion in an old boys' network or alumni association might even be desirable. Where there seems to be total dedication to the institution with no worries about other claims, it is probably when it is seen as 'not so much a programme, more a way of life',[1] and this is not necessarily the best way to further its purpose, especially in times of change. For organizations and institutions exist for purposes besides providing a way of life for those who participate in them (though this is sometimes forgotten, as by those who lamented that their Home for unmarried mothers might be closed for lack of girls needing help). We have here something of a dilemma; if an organization becomes a way of life, people get a vested interest in maintaining it as it is. But unless it holds the loyalty of its participants in maintaining its character as an institution, its serious purposes will suffer. This has been brought out well by Philip Selznick in *Leadership and Administration*; indeed he distinguishes 'organization' and 'institution' on this score. An organization can be a mobilization of energies for a special purpose. If it is to stand up and last, it must also be an institution, i.e. a community of people with the conflicts and adjustments this will involve, so that its leadership is a *political* and not just a technical task.[2] (Selznick is very good

major method of control is through coercion; those where it is utilitarian, through calculation of interests (especially remuneration), and those where it is 'normative' through moral involvement of participants in the organization.

[1] The title of a feature current on B.B.C. Television at the time of writing.

[2] I note this way of distinguishing 'organizations' and 'institutions' and saying how they overlap. In this chapter I have been concerned with organizations which are also institutions in Selznick's sense, and have sometimes called them 'institutions'. Since, however, the word 'institution' is also used by sociologists for such things as marriage or property, I prefer in general to call specific corporate bodies 'organizations'.

on this; he does not, however, discuss the question of limits of commitment.)

Moreover the purposes of organizations can be very different, in that they may be 'diffuse' or 'specific' as Talcott Parsons would say, and they may touch the lives of their participants at many points or at few. One way of distinguishing organizations could be in terms of the kinds of purposes they serve, and by asking how possible it is to define them operationally.

1. There are organizations whose general purpose is sufficiently specific for it to be tolerably easy to define how it could be operational, though of course this does not mean it is easy to implement it. For instance if the purpose of a firm is to survive and make a profit, the existence of bankruptcy courts and balance sheets can provide evidence of success and failure. 'Operational' here means the possibility of citing what would count as empirical evidence of success or failure; as well as showing how the purpose might be implemented through relating its general statement to a number of interlocking functional activities. In these cases the values of efficiency and inefficiency can also be judged (if not measured) in relation to empirically defined conditions of success or failure. Yet even here, underlying these clearly operational values, there will be the more general aim of maintaining the integrity of the organization as an institution, and what this entails will need continual rethinking in changing circumstances.

2. There are organizations whose general purpose is very difficult to state succinctly, and which may even be a matter of some controversy. A university is a case in point. One can say 'education and research', and there will be arguments about which has priority; 'the advancement of knowledge', and then the scales seem to be weighted in favour of research, and it can be asked whether other kinds of institutes for advanced studies may not concentrate more effectively on this. An older generation put the purpose

explicitly in a social and religious context: 'that there may not be lacking a succession of persons duly qualified for the service of God in Church and State'. It is doubtful whether in these days there can be a single clear and agreed statement of purpose, and still more doubtful whether this can be made operational by any precise tests. The attempt to do so is likely to fasten attention on the more obviously measurable output — numbers of publications, or of students, or of high Honours degrees. 'It is what they are in ten years' time that matters', Whitehead quoted someone as saying of undergraduates. By that time the university will have lost track of most of them. So indices of success and failure are likely to be misleading.

This does not mean we are completely in the dark about whether such an organization is a good instance of its kind or not. It has been said that a university may be judged by the number of intelligent enthusiasms it fosters. But these may wax and wane with the coming and going of particular personalities; a university may be strong in one thing at one time and another at another. Thus we must make a broad distinction between the kinds of organization in which there is a common purpose which can be implemented through a large number of functional contributions under division of labour with measurable indices of success, and organizations where the purpose is more elusive, and comes to life in differing emphases where the organization provides opportunities for people to do jobs which can only be done creatively if they are free to do them very much in their own way.[1] Such jobs are 'vocational' in the old sense of work done from incentives in a person's own internal springs of action, and where opportunity to do the work

[1] The evidence cited in an earlier chapter (see p. 133) of how the integrity of teachers in colleges of high quality in America was protected by the administration, when they were under accusations during the McCarthy crisis, is an example of a good mutual reinforcement of different roles in an organization.

matters more than the exact ticket under which it is done. Yet under contemporary conditions a vocationally minded person generally has to work in and with the resources of a large organization. Scientific discoveries, for instance, are now seldom made in the shed at the bottom of the garden; they need laboratories with expensive equipment and access to considerable funds. This is likely to involve a vocationally minded researcher, especially in times of change and development, in the political processes of communication and decision making. It is at least arguable that he might have more freedom to do his own special kind of work under the conditions of a benevolent and loose kind of autocracy — tempered by what Samuel Alexander, addressing the Registrar of the University of Manchester of the day (about 1926), called 'the affectionate insubordination which characterizes our relations with our administrative colleagues'. But no doubt this happy semblance of anarchy goes with a stable state of affairs where not many policy decisions are necessary. In times of change and growth, the demand for a more democratic system of formal and not only informal participation is natural, but as we have noted it is likely to consume a good deal of people's time and energy, especially as these processes can become absorbing through their own fascination. If in the end of the day the chief concentration is to be on the main job rather than on the mainspring of the mechanism for doing it, or even on the main chance, some countervailing measures may be necessary; for instance, readiness to allow a fairly wide discretion to those on whom certain kinds of decision may be devolved, for instance where time is an important factor. Otherwise vocational man may find himself ousted by organization man, or making a vocation out of being organization man. For some people no doubt this is as it should be; to make it general, is surely to produce a confusion of ends and means.

'A confusion of ends and means.' Organizations and

their politics can become a way of life, and increasingly so where those doing the substantive work for which they have been set up are also drawn into the work of running them. No doubt in a democratic age up to a point this is as it should be. Yet there are distinctions. I have noted the need both for loyalty to institutions and for freedom of spirit over against them, and what I have said about the complexity of ethical problems and the conflicts of roles, public, private and professional, which are endemic to organizations, may seem cold comfort to those who have to live with them. Yet we need to be able to see complexity and to go on thinking without falling into Utopianism or cynicism. 'Seek simplicity and distrust it' — a maxim of Whitehead's — can be a guide so long as we see that among the simplicities to be distrusted is the ideological pursuit of a single ideal or principle without realistic appraisal of its implications in a particular setting. These may be such as to produce consequences of a kind which boomerang back on to the original ideal, frustrating it or leading to a swing from Utopianism to cynicism.[1] But the other extreme is an opportunism which neither carries moral respect nor is likely to be compatible with policy making. We come back to a view of moral judgment as neither simply rule-directed nor simply calculation of consequences, but needing to take responsible account of both. It has indeed the guiding lights of fairness and sympathy — the marks of practical reason in morality — but these may have to be brought to bear on a complex tangle of interests to be considered or reconciled. To meet this complexity calls not only for disinterestedness but for intelligence.

[1] See above, p. 198, for Selznick's diagnosis in *T.V.A. and the Grass Roots* of the effects of the pursuit of the principle of local participation. Also Merton's observations on conditions where an ideal can be frustrated by unanticipated consequences in 'The Unanticipated Consequences of Purposive Social Action', and also 'The Boomerang Response' (cf. above, pp. 126 and 117).

Failure to see complexity can feed tensions between those whose primary responsibility is to keep the organization or institution going and those whose primary interest is an ideal, a principle or the claims of a specific piece of work. In my preface I said that I might have dedicated this book to administrators whose hearts are with the anarchists and to anarchists who have a heart for the administrators. There are those who will want to go all out for an idea, a principle, the possibilities of a creative piece of work. There are also those concerned with ways and means, and the repercussions of the pursuit of one idea or interest on others. These will be likely to set a high value on stability, since they have the responsibility of seeing that departures from recognized procedures do not pass certain limits, and that if possible the organization survives. They will be tempted to avoid people who will be 'difficult' or who may 'rock the boat'—and there is probably a bit of an anarchist in most people of high originality. The temptation of the latter is to see the administrators as 'bureaucrats' (used as a dirty word) more interested in perpetuating the organization and their own power in it than in the real work. Both may sometimes be right; but not always. Even where they are not right, there is likely to be tension. Tension is easier to live with where we can see the reasons for it, and, above all, where each kind of person can know at bottom that he needs and depends on the other. It is no small gain if there is something in a person of the one kind which responds to concerns more often found in the other: an administrator may be a poet on the side, and an inventor or writer may have known what it is like to have a share in government.[1] Nevertheless, as St. Paul told us, there are

---

[1] Plato warned us that we should only trust rulers who held office unwillingly. He went too far, since most things are better done by those who enjoy doing them. But he had a point: we can mistrust politicians and administrators who are only interested in politics and administration.

diversities of gifts. St. Paul also spoke of a body in which there is mutual dependence of different members and functions. In a general way, this perception has come to us from our Christian tradition.[1] We need realistic and detailed understanding of ways in which these mutual dependences work, and here perhaps sociologists can help us with their interest in diagnosing multiple relationships. The point was seen by Roger Wilson, writing of Friends' Relief Work after the last war.[2] That organization was a good laboratory for the purpose, since it was set up for work which in the nature of the case attracts a number of potentially anarchic characters — 'conscientious objectors' often not only to military service but to any kind of authority. He writes of how they found that 'ordinary' and 'extraordinary' personalities were necessary to each other and could build one another up.[3] 'For outstanding individuals are not by any means always very well balanced. Imagination often resides in those with intense inner conflicts; drive in those who lack a sense of personal inner security; inspiration in those who are careless about details; capacity for understanding people in those who do not mind much about administration; administrative ability in those who think along well-set lines. Sometimes, of course, people do emerge with exceptional qualities in the desired mixture, but ability is wasted if it cannot be used when lop-sided.

[1] It was something which the late Charles Williams saw; it runs through his novels, and also his books *The Descent of the Dove* and *The Figure of Beatrice*, under the themes of 'coinherence' and 'exchange'.

[2] *Authority, Leadership and Concern* (Swarthmore Lecture, 1949), p. 21.

[3] In commenting on this observation in my *Function, Purpose and Powers* (p. 263), I remarked that the 'ordinary' people who help build up a society in which they do not exasperate the 'extraordinary' people but help them to find constructive expression for their ideas, are not likely to be as ordinary as all that. I also discussed this question of the relations between different kinds of 'vocational' characters.

The more intelligently stable the group temperament, the more readily can exceptional abilities find useful and constructive scope for their expression.'[1] Intelligent stability might be taken as epitomizing one administrative aim. To achieve it can be a difficult, creative task needing all the ability and moral toughness that Chester Barnard has said that it needs. And yet, at the same time, it is a means and not an end. Administrators need the self-abnegation of putting high ability and indeed powers of leadership into providing opportunities for other people to do something else.

Not only so within the work of an organization ; this is a fact also about the wider life of society, not seen by those to whom keeping some sort of stable framework of life going just appears as one of the ways in which the 'establishment' tries to hold on to its power. Yet not only artists and others who do first-hand work of the kind which wins social recognition depend on the people who 'maintain the fabric of the world';[2] so too do those who try to contract out of society — the would-be anarchists and beats, and those who talk about 'alienation'. Their dependence is not only true in the trivial logical sense in which no one can be a rebel without something to rebel against (which is a trivial point, even when dressed up in Hegelian language about 'negation'). It is true as a practical empirical point, since we all depend on a background of routines being carried out, services maintained, basic securities provided, and so assume the existence of a host of people who are prepared to take the responsibilities of their parts in this. Spontaneity and creativity need a framework; they are not likely to flourish in social chaos. And this goes for the social rebel as well as for the original genius. One *avant-garde* pop singer, Roger Miller, has seen this.

1 *Authority, Leadership and Concern*, p. 21.
2 Ecclesiasticus, xxxviii, 4.

'Squares make the world go round.
Sounds profane, sounds profound.
But government cain't be made do
By hipsters wearing rope-soled shoes.'[1]

This is not only a bid for tolerance, a way of saying that it takes all sorts to make a world. It means that we see how different kinds of temperament and capacity — those who produce protest, and those who produce original work, and those who produce stability — need one another, and depend on one another.

Yet, as psychologists and novelists have always known, dependence is an ambivalent relation which produces its tensions. These can best be carried when we see the reasons for them, and in our modern society some of these reasons may lie in the nature of large organizations. In these *milieux* people meet each other not only as carrying out complementary functions (as they may well do), but at the same time occupying multiple and potentially conflicting roles. This is something which cannot be wished away or organized away; it is a fact of life to be understood and lived with.

Anthony Sampson in *The Anatomy of Britain* quotes from Bagehot, 'The characteristic danger of great nations, like the Roman or the English, which have a long history of continuous creation, is that they may at last fail from not comprehending the great institutions they have created'.[2] It is a merit of Sampson's book that he sees that to understand contemporary Britain we must look at what is happening in its large organizations — the Civil Service, political parties, schools and universities, business corporations. We need a number of imaginative and well-documented sociological studies of these; it should not be left to journalists with historical and sociological sense to do most

---

[1] Quoted in *Time* Magazine, March 19, 1965.
[2] *Anatomy of Britain* (London, 1962), p. 638.

of the work. For if I am right, it is these big organizations which increasingly dominate contemporary society, and which are producing some of the most difficult and insistent moral problems we have to face. The sociologist may not just be, as Professor Sprott has suggested, 'the specialist who tries to elaborate and make precise the administrative world picture'.[1] But at least his training in studying role behaviour in networks of social relations should give him some expertise in helping us to understand a world in which administrative, executive and professional action, rather than the individual ways of the amateur, is increasingly dominant.

Organization Man need not swallow up all our life. Yet Whyte's grim diagnosis of how he may swallow up our moral initiative may well prove true if we do not see how the complex moral problems of institutionalized life, just because they are impersonal as well as personal, call for more intelligence in diagnosis and more resource in moral judgment and moral courage than do those of a purely personal morality. The trouble is that though their impersonal side does call for this, it can also be invoked to allow responsibility to be evaded,[2] and the evasion can be encouraged by a popular deterministic interpretation of the findings of the social sciences. This need not be our conclusion; indeed to look further into what these can tell us, and to look behind it, may help towards a better appreciation of the person in the *persona* rather than his defacement. It will point to rules of social morality as guides rather than as determinants of judgment, of roles as played with individual style, and of social relations as relations which are

[1] *Science and Social Action* (London, 1954), p. 17.
[2] Anthony Sampson also writes, 'This, surely, is the greater nightmare of a democracy — not that the government is full of sinister and all-powerful *éminences grises*, but that the will of the people dissolves itself in committees, with thousands of men murmuring about their duty to "those whom we serve"'. (*Ibid.* p. 627.)

still between human beings even though at many degrees of indirectness.

Moralists and sociologists may have different professional interests in these problems and the kinds of conflicts they present. To write perceptively about these they need not abrogate their special interests; but they could well be less concerned with demarcating frontiers, and more concerned with joint exploration of the no-man's-land in which we live our moral predicaments.

INDEX

Adkins, A. W. H., 83 n.
Alexander, S., 208
Anomie, 130
Anscombe, E., 111–12
Aristotle, 5, 11, 60, 69, 79, 86, 97, 155, 170
Arnold, Dr. T., 140
Austin, J. L., 120 n.
Autonomy of ethics, 2, 33, 36 ff., 53–55, 82, 109

Bagehot, W., 203, 213
Baier, K., 12 n.
Bales, R. F., 97 n., 157 n.
Barber, Elinor, 160 n.
Barnard, Chester, 165–6, 200–1, 212
Barnard College, vii
Beausobre, Julia de, 123
Benedict, Ruth, 102–3, 136
Benn, S. I., 86 n.
Bentham, J., 85, 187
Bergson, H., 180
Bettelheim, B., 123
Black, M., 12 n.
Boomerang effect, 117, 209 n.
Boorstin, D., 175 n.
Bosanquet, B., 181
Boulton, W. W., 162 n.
Bowen, Elinor Smith, 24 n.
Bradley, F. H., 181
Braithwaite, R. B., 87, 123, 124 n.
Brandt, R., 31, 32, 59, 65 n., 73, 74, 76, 84 n.
Brown, R., 124 n.
Bureaucracy, 185 ff., 191, 194, 204
Burke, E., 105, 204
Burns, T., vii, 185, 188–9, 194–6
Butler, J., 11, 64 n.

Carritt, E. F., 87
Casuistry, 50–52
Christianity, 177, 199, 211
Coleman, S., vii
Columbia University, vii, 160
Consequences, intended and unintended, 3, 125, 126, 129, 197 ff., 209
— moral relevance of, 51, 52
Cultural anthropology, 136

Dalton, Melville, 173 n., 192
Davis, Kingsley, 128

Denning L.J., 80
Deontic Logic, 84 n.
Determinism and freewill, 109, 114 ff., 121
Devons, E., 141 n.
Dewey, John, 29
Dobu, 102–3
Dostoevsky, F. M., 117
Draper, Ruth, 140
Duncan Jones, A., 64 n.
Duncker, K., 94 n.
Durkheim, E., 9, 103–4, 106, 127, 130

Edel, A., 31, 75 n., 95–96
Edel, May, 31 n., 75 n., 95–96
Edwards, Paul, 37 n.
Edwards, Quenton, 161 n.
Eichmann, A., 204
Emmet, Dorothy, 14 n., 72 n., 79 n., 101 n., 128 n., 142 n., 172 n., 211 n.
Epictetus, 178
Epiphany Philosophers, vii
Equity, 79, 107
Ethical systems, 31–32
— theory, 32, 82 ff., 99. *See also* Autonomy of ethics
Ethics, substantive, see *Mores*; Judgment, moral
Etzioni, A., 204 n.
Evans-Pritchard, E. E., 102
Existentialism, 61, 63, 78, 147, 152, 154–5, 171
Explanation, kinds of, 112, 123–4
— psychological, 120 ff., 141
— sociological, 111, 125 ff. *See also* Structural-functional explanations

Farrer, Austin, 115
Feedback, 113, 129, 193
Feiffer, 156
Finch, H. A., 17 n.
Findlay, J. A., 118
Firth, R., 65 n., 73
Flanders and Swann, 104
Flew, Antony, 42 n.
Follett, Mary P., 195
Foot, P., 53 n.
Fortes, M., 140, 147
Fortune, Rheo, 102, 103
Freud, S., 157